Personality Types

Marie-Louise von Franz, Honorary Patron

**Studies in Jungian Psychology
by Jungian Analysts**

Daryl Sharp, General Editor

PERSONALITY TYPES

Jung's Model of Typology

DARYL SHARP

To my mother and father and to Vicki and Jessie

Appendix 2, "The Clinical Significance of Extraversion and
Introversion," by H.K. Fierz, M.D., is reproduced here by
permission of Antoinette Fierz of Zurich and Daimon Verlag
of Einsiedeln, Switzerland, publisher of the late Dr. Fierz's papers.

Canadian Cataloguing in Publication Data
Sharp, Daryl, 1936-
    Personality types: Jung's model of typology

(Studies in Jungian psychology by Jungian analysts; 31)

Includes bibliographical references and index.

ISBN 0-919123-30-9

1. Personality. 2. Typology (Psychology). 3. Jung,
C.G. (Carl Gustav), 1875-1961. I. Title. II. Series.

BF698.S48 1987   155.2'64   C87-095102-5

INNER CITY BOOKS
Box 1271, Station Q, Toronto, ON M4T 2P4, Canada
Telephone (416) 927-0355 / Fax (416) 924-1814
Web site: www.innercitybooks.net / E-mail: admin@innercitybooks.net

Honorary Patron: Marie-Louise von Franz.
Publisher and General Editor: Daryl Sharp.
Senior Editor: Victoria Cowan.

INNER CITY BOOKS was founded in 1980 to promote the
understanding and practical application of the work of C.G. Jung.

Cover painting by Jessie Kate Cowan-Sharp.

Printed and bound in Canada by University of Toronto Press Incorporated

CONTENTS

See final pages for descriptions of other Inner City Books

*Classification does not explain the
individual psyche. Nevertheless, an understanding of
psychological types opens the way to a better
understanding of human psychology in general.*

—C.G. Jung.

Preface

This book is not a critique or a defence of the model of psychological types elaborated by C.G. Jung, but rather an explanation. The intention here is not to simplify the model, but to illustrate its complexity and some of its practical implications.

Jung's model of typology is not a system of character analysis, nor is it a way of labeling oneself or others. Much as one might use a compass to determine where one is in the physical world, Jung's typology is a tool for psychological orientation. It is a way of understanding both oneself and the interpersonal difficulties that arise between people.

Other books have been written based on Jung's system of psychological types. If there is anything distinctive about this one, it is its close adherence to Jung's expressed views.

Jung in 1959, at the age of 84

1

Introduction to Jungian Typology

The experience that not everyone functions in the same way has been the basis for numerous systems of typology. From earliest times attempts have been made to categorize individual attitudes and behavior patterns, in order to explain the differences between people.

The oldest system of typology known to us is the one devised by oriental astrologers. They classified character in terms of four trigons, corresponding to the four elements—water, air, earth and fire. The air trigon in the horoscope, for instance, consists of the three aerial signs of the zodiac, Aquarius, Gemini, Libra; the fire trigon is made up of Aries, Leo and Sagittarius. According to this age-old view, whoever is born under these signs shares in their aerial or fiery nature and has a corresponding temperament and fate; similarly for the water and earth signs. This system survives in modified form in present-day astrology.

Closely connected with this ancient cosmological scheme is the physiological typology of Greek medicine, according to which individuals were classified as phlegmatic, sanguine, choleric or melancholic, based on the designations for the secretions of the body (phlegm, blood, yellow bile and black bile). These descriptions are still in common linguistic use, though medically they have long since been superseded.

Jung's own model of typology grew out of an extensive historical review of the type question in literature, mythology, aesthetics, philosophy and psychopathology. In the preface to *Psychological Types,* which contains his scholarly research and a detailed summary of his conclusions, he writes:

This book is the fruit of nearly twenty years' work in the domain of practical psychology. It grew gradually in my thoughts, taking shape from the countless impressions and experiences of a psychiatrist in the treatment of nervous illnesses, from intercourse with men and women of all social levels, from my personal dealings with friend and foe alike, and, finally, from a critique of my own psychological peculiarities.[1]

The Basic Model

Whereas the earlier classifications were based on observations of temperamental or emotional behavior patterns, Jung's model is concerned with the movement of psychic energy and the way in which one habitually or preferentially orients oneself in the world.

From this point of view, Jung differentiates eight typological groups: *two personality attitudes*—introversion and extraversion—and *four functions or modes of orientation*—thinking, sensation, intuition and feeling—each of which may operate in an introverted or extraverted way.

The resulting eight variations will be examined in later chapters, with detailed descriptions of how each of the functions appears in combination with either the extraverted or introverted attitude. What follows here is a brief explanation of the terms Jung used. Although introversion and extraversion have become household words, their meaning is frequently misunderstood; the four functions are not so widely known, and even less understood.

---

[1] *Psychological Types*, CW 6, p. xi. [CW refers throughout to *The Collected Works of C.G. Jung* (Bollingen Series XX), 20 vols., trans. R.F.C. Hull, ed. H. Read, M. Fordham, G. Adler, Wm. McGuire; Princeton: Princeton University Press, 1953-1979.]

Introversion and extraversion are psychological modes of adaptation. In the former, the movement of energy is toward the inner world. In the latter, interest is directed toward the outer world. In one case the subject (inner reality) and in the other the object (things and other people, outer reality) is of primary importance.

Introversion, writes Jung, "is normally characterized by a hesitant, reflective, retiring nature that keeps itself to itself, shrinks from objects [and] is always slightly on the defensive."[2]

Conversely, *extraversion* "is normally characterized by an outgoing, candid, and accommodating nature that adapts easily to a given situation, quickly forms attachments, and, setting aside any possible misgivings, will often venture forth with careless confidence into unknown situations."[3]

In the extraverted attitude, external factors are the predominant motivating force for judgments, perceptions, feelings, affects and actions. This sharply contrasts with the psychological nature of introversion, where internal or subjective factors are the chief motivation.

Extraverts like to travel, meet new people, see new places. They are the typical adventurers, the life of the party, open and friendly. The introvert is essentially conservative, preferring the familiar surroundings of home, intimate times with a few close friends. To the extravert, the introvert is a stick-in-the mud, a spoil-sport, dull and predictable. Conversely, the introvert, who tends to be more self-sufficient than the extravert, might describe the latter as flighty, a superficial gad-about.

In practice, it is not possible to demonstrate the introverted and extraverted attitudes per se, that is in isolation. Whether a person is one way or the other only becomes apparent in asso-

---

2 *Two Essays on Analytical Psychology,* CW 7, par. 62.
3 Ibid.

ciation with one of the four functions, each of which has its special area of expertise.

The function of *thinking* refers to the process of cognitive thought, *sensation* is perception by means of the physical sense organs, *feeling* is the function of subjective judgment or valuation, and *intuition* refers to perception by way of the unconscious (e.g., receptivity to unconscious contents).

Jung's basic model, including the relationship between the four functions, is a quaternity, as shown in the diagram below. Thinking is here arbitrarily placed at the top; any of the other functions might be placed there, according to which one a person most favors. The relative position of the other functions, however—which one is at the bottom and which two on the horizontal axis—are determined by the one at the top. The reason for this, involving the nature of the individual functions, will soon become apparent.

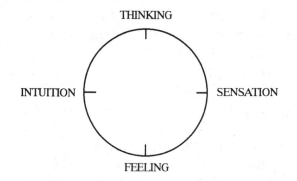

Briefly, the sensation function establishes that something exists, thinking tells us what it is, feeling tells us what it's worth, and through intuition we have a sense of what can be done with it (the possibilities). Any one function by itself is not sufficient for ordering our experience of ourselves or the world around us; all four, writes Jung, are required for a comprehensive understanding:

For complete orientation all four functions should con-
tribute equally: thinking should facilitate cognition and
judgment, feeling should tell us how and to what extent a
thing is important or unimportant for us, sensation should
convey concrete reality to us through seeing, hearing, tast-
ing, etc., and intuition should enable us to divine the hidden possibilities in the background, since these too belong
to the complete picture of a given situation.[4]

The ideal of course is to have conscious access to the
function or functions required or appropriate for particular
circumstances, but in practice the four functions are not
equally at one's conscious disposal; that is, they are not uniformly developed or differentiated in any individual. Invariably one or the other is more developed, called the primary or
superior function, while the rest remain inferior, relatively
undifferentiated.

The terms "superior" and "inferior" in this context do not
imply value judgments. No function is any better than any of
the others. The superior function is simply the one a person is
most likely to use; similarly, inferior does not mean pathological but merely unused (or at least less used compared to the
favored function).

What happens to those functions that are not consciously
brought into daily use and therefore not developed?

They remain in a more or less primitive and infantile state,
often only half conscious, or even quite unconscious. The
relatively undeveloped functions constitute a specific inferiority which is characteristic of each type and is an in-
tegral part of his total character. The one-sided emphasis on

---

[4] *Psychological Types,* CW 6, par. 900. Jung acknowledged that the four
orienting functions do not contain everything in the conscious psyche.
Will power and memory, for instance, are not included. The reason for
this is that they are not typological determinants—though naturally they
may be affected by the way one functions typologically.

thinking is always accompanied by an inferiority of feeling, and differentiated sensation is injurious to intuition and vice versa.[5]

Typologically, many people are a bowl of soup. They function in an introverted or extraverted way depending on their mood, the weather or their state of mind; they think, feel, sense and intuit more or less at random, being no better or worse at one function than any other, and having no inkling of the consequences.

Such people may at first glance seem to be well rounded. However, the above characteristics are typical of unconsciousness, for consciousness implies a certain differentiation in the way one functions. "The uniformly conscious or uniformly unconscious state of the functions," notes Jung, "is the mark of a primitive mentality."[6]

Rational and Irrational Functions

Jung further described two of the four functions as *rational* and two as *irrational.* (He also used the terms *judging* and *perceiving,* respectively.)

Thinking, as a function of logical discrimination, is rational (judging). So is feeling, which as a way of evaluating our likes and dislikes can be quite as discriminating as thinking. Thinking and feeling are called rational because both are based on a reflective, linear process that coalesces into a particular judgment.

Sensation and intuition Jung called irrational (perceiving) functions. Each is a way of perceiving simply what is—sensation sees what is in the external world, intuition sees (or we might say "picks up") what is in the inner world.

---

[5] Ibid., par. 955.

[6] Ibid., par. 667.

The term "irrational," as applied to the functions of sensation and intuition, does not mean illogical or unreasonable, but rather beyond or outside of reason. The physical perception of something does not depend on logic—things just *are.* Similarly, an intuition exists in itself; it is present in the mind, independent of reason or a rational process of thought. Jung comments:

> Merely because [the irrational types] subordinate judgment to perception, it would be quite wrong to regard them as "unreasonable." It would be truer to say that they are in the highest degree *empirical.* They base themselves exclusively on experience—so exclusively that, as a rule, their judgment cannot keep pace with their experience.[7]

It is particularly important to distinguish between feeling as a psychological function and the many other common uses of the word. Jung acknowledged the possible confusion: we say we feel happy, sad, angry, regretful, and so on; we have a feeling the weather will change or the stock market will fall; silk feels smoother than burlap, something doesn't feel right, etc. Clearly we use the word feeling quite loosely, since in a particular context it may refer to sense perception, thoughts, intuition or an emotional reaction.

Here it is a matter of clearly defining our terminology. We can measure temperature according to degrees Fahrenheit, Celsius or Réaumur, distance in miles or kilometers, weight in ounces or grams, bulk in cups, bushels or pounds—so long as we indicate which system we are using. In Jung's model, the term feeling refers strictly to the way in which we subjectively evaluate what something, or someone, is worth to us. This is the sense in which it is rational; in fact, to the extent that it is not colored by emotion, which is to say influenced by an activated complex, feeling can be quite cold.

---

[7] Ibid., par. 371.

Indeed, the feeling function, as a mode of psychological orientation, must above all not be confused with emotion. The latter, more properly called affect, is invariably the consequence of an active complex. "Feeling is distinguished from affect," writes Jung, "by the fact that it produces no perceptible physical innervations, i.e., neither more nor less than an ordinary thinking process."[8]

Affect tends to contaminate or distort each of the functions: we can't think straight when we are mad; happiness colors the way we perceive things and people; we can't properly evaluate what something is worth to us when we're upset; and possibilities dry up when we're depressed.

The Primary Function and Auxiliary Functions

As noted above, one of the four functions is invariably more developed than the others. This is the primary or superior function, the one we automatically use because it comes most naturally and brings certain rewards. Writes Jung:

> Experience shows that it is practically impossible, owing to adverse circumstances in general, for anyone to develop all his psychological functions simultaneously. The demands of society compel a man to apply himself first and foremost to the differentiation of the function with which he is best equipped by nature, or which will secure him the greatest social success. Very frequently, indeed as a general rule, a man identifies more or less completely with the most favoured and hence the most developed function. It is this that gives rise to the various psychological types. As a consequence of this one-sided development, one or more functions are necessarily retarded.[9]

---

[8] Ibid., par. 725.
[9] Ibid., par. 763.

The word "retarded" here simply means neglected or not well developed. In fact only in extreme cases are the other functions completely absent, and there is regularly a second function (occasionally even a third) that is prominent enough to exert a co-determining influence on consciousness.

One can of course be conscious of the contents or products associated with each of the functions. For instance, I can know what I'm thinking without having a primary thinking function, and I can tell the difference between a table and a bottle without having a superior sensation function. But we can only speak of the "consciousness" of a function, according to Jung, "when its use is under the control of the will and, at the same time, its governing principle is the decisive one for the orientation of consciousness":

> This absolute sovereignty always belongs, empirically, to one function alone, and *can* belong only to one function, because the equally independent intervention of another function would necessarily produce a different orientation which, partially at least, would contradict the first. But since it is a vital condition for the conscious process of adaptation always to have clear and unambiguous aims, the presence of a second function of equal power is naturally ruled out. This other function, therefore, can have only a secondary importance. . . . Its secondary importance is due to the fact that it is not, like the primary function . . . an absolutely reliable and decisive factor, but comes into play more as an auxiliary or complementary function.[10]

In practice, the auxiliary function is always one whose nature, rational or irrational, is different from the primary function. For instance, feeling cannot be the secondary function when thinking is dominant, and vice versa, because both are rational or judging functions:

---

[10] Ibid., par. 667.

Thinking, if it is to be real thinking and true to its own principle, must rigorously exclude feeling. This, of course, does not do away with the the fact that there are individuals whose thinking and feeling are on the same level, both being of equal motive power for consciousness. But in these cases there is also no question of a differentiated type, but merely of relatively undeveloped thinking and feeling.[11]

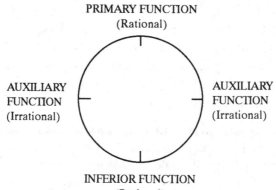

PRIMARY FUNCTION
(Rational)

AUXILIARY FUNCTION (Irrational)

AUXILIARY FUNCTION (Irrational)

INFERIOR FUNCTION
(Rational)

The secondary function is therefore always one whose nature differs from, but is not antagonistic to, the primary function: either of the irrational functions can be auxiliary to one of the rational functions, and vice versa.

Similarly, when sensation is the primary function, intuition cannot be the auxiliary function, and vice versa. This is because the effective operation of sensation demands that it focus on sense perceptions in the outer world. This is not simultaneously compatible with intuition, which "senses" what is happening in the inner world.

Thus thinking and intuition can readily pair, as can thinking and sensation, since the nature of intuition and sensation is

---

[11] Ibid.

not fundamentally opposed to the thinking function. Indeed, as we will see later in detailed descriptions of the types, either intuition or sensation, both being irrational functions of perception, would be very helpful to the rational judgments of the thinking function.

It is equally true in practice that sensation is bolstered by the auxiliary function of thinking or feeling, feeling is aided by sensation or intuition, and intuition by feeling or thinking.

> The resulting combinations present the familiar picture of, for instance, practical thinking allied with sensation, speculative thinking forging ahead with intuition, artistic intuition selecting and presenting its images with the help of feeling-values, philosophical intuition systematizing its vision into comprehensive thought by means of a powerful intellect, and so on.[12]

The Inferior Function

As already mentioned, those functions other than the one most dominant, most preferred, are relatively inferior.

In all cases, there is one function which particularly resists integration into consciousness. This is called the inferior function, or sometimes, to distinguish it from the other inferior functions, "the fourth function."

"The essence of the inferior function," writes Jung, "is autonomy: it is independent, it attacks, it fascinates and so spins us about that we are no longer masters of ourselves and can no longer rightly distinguish between ourselves and others."[13]

Marie-Louise von Franz, Jung's close colleague and collaborator for many years, points out that one of the great

---

[12] Ibid., par. 669.

[13] *Two Essays,* par. 85.

problems of the inferior function is that it is generally slow, in contrast with the primary function:

> [That is why] people hate to start work on it; the reaction of the superior function comes out quickly and well adapted, while many people have no idea where their inferior function really is. For instance, thinking types have no idea whether they have feeling or what kind of feeling it is. They have to sit half an hour and meditate as to whether they have feelings about something and, if so, what they are. If you ask a thinking type what he feels, he generally either replies with a thought or gives a quick conventional reaction; and if you then insist on knowing what he really feels, he does not know. Pulling it up from his belly, so to speak, can take half an hour. Or, if an intuitive fills out a tax form he needs a week where other people would take a day.[14]

In Jung's model, as shown in the diagram on page 20, the inferior or fourth function is invariably of the same nature as the primary function: when the rational function of thinking is most developed, then the other rational function, feeling, will be inferior; if sensation is dominant, then intuition, the other irrational function, will be the fourth function, and so on.

This accords with general experience: the thinker is regularly tripped up by feeling values; the practical sensation type easily gets into a rut, blind to the possibilities "seen" by intuition; the feeling type is deaf to the conclusions presented by logical thinking; and the intuitive, tuned into the inner world, runs afoul of concrete reality.

One is not necessarily completely oblivious to those perceptions or judgments associated with the inferior function. Thinking types, for example, may know their feelings—inso-

---

[14] *Lectures on Jung's Typology* (Zurich: Spring Publications, 1971), p. 8.

far as they are capable of introspection[15]—but they do not give them much weight; they will deny their validity and may even claim they are not influenced by them.

Similarly, sensation types who are one-sidedly oriented to physical sense perceptions may have intuitions, but even if they recognize them they will not be motivated by them. Likewise, feeling types will brush away disturbing thoughts and intuitives will simply ignore what is right in front of their face.

Although the inferior function may be conscious as a phenomenon its true significance nevertheless remains unrecognized. It behaves like many repressed or insufficiently appreciated contents, which are partly conscious and partly unconscious . . . . Thus in normal cases the inferior function remains conscious, at least in its effects; but in a neurosis it sinks wholly or in part into the unconscious.[16]

To the extent that a person functions too one-sidedly, the inferior function becomes correspondingly primitive and troublesome, both to oneself and to others. ("Life has no mercy," notes von Franz, "with the inferiority of the inferior function.")[17] The psychic energy claimed by the primary function takes energy away from the inferior function, which falls into the unconscious. There it is prone to be activated in an unnatural way, giving rise to infantile fantasies and a variety of personality disturbances.

This is what regularly happens in a so-called mid-life crisis, when an individual has neglected aspects of the person-

---

[15] The difference between introversion and introspection is that the former refers to the direction in which energy moves, while the latter refers to self-examination. Although the capacity for introspection—which Jung calls "self-communing" (see below, pages 38 and 69)—does seem to be more prevalent among introverts, neither the introverted attitude nor the thinking function has a monopoly on introspection.

[16] *Psychological Types,* CW 6, par. 764.

[17] *Jung's Typology,* p. 12.

ality for so long that they finally demand to be recognized. At such times it is usual to project the cause of the "disturbances" onto others. But only a period of self-reflection and analysis of the fantasies can restore the balance and make further development possible. Indeed, as von Franz points out, a crisis of this kind can be a golden opportunity:

> In the realm of the inferior function there is a great concentration of life, so that as soon as the superior function is worn out—begins to rattle and lose oil like an old car—if people succeed in turning to their inferior function, they will rediscover a new potential of life. Everything in the realm of the inferior function becomes exciting, dramatic, full of positive and negative possibilities. There is tremendous tension and the world is, as it were, rediscovered through the inferior function.[18]

—not, however, without some discomfort, for the process of assimilating the inferior function, "raising" it into consciousness, is invariably accompanied by a "lowering" of the superior or primary function.

The thinking type who concentrates on the feeling function, for instance, has trouble writing an essay, can't think logically; the sensation type actively involved with intuition loses keys, forgets appointments, leaves the stove on overnight; the intuitive becomes fascinated with sound, color, texture, and ignores possibilities; the feeling type burrows into books, immersed in ideas to the detriment of a social life. In each case, the problem becomes one of finding a middle way.

There are typical characteristics associated with each function when it operates in an inferior way. Some of these are discussed later. Here it is sufficient to note that oversensitivity and strong emotional reactions of any kind—from falling in love to blind rage—are a sure sign that the inferior function,

---

[18] Ibid., p. 11.

along with one or more complexes, has been activated. This naturally gives rise to a multitude of relationship problems.

In therapy, when it becomes desirable or necessary to develop the inferior function, this can only happen gradually, and by first going through one of the auxiliary functions. As Jung comments:

> I have frequently observed how an analyst, confronted with a terrific thinking type, for instance, will do his utmost to develop the feeling function directly out of the unconscious. Such an attempt is foredoomed to failure, because it involves too great a violation of the conscious standpoint. Should the violation nevertheless be successful, a really compulsive dependence of the patient on the analyst ensues, a transference that can only be brutally terminated, because, having been left without a standpoint, the patient has made his standpoint the analyst. . . . In order to cushion the impact of the unconscious, an irrational type needs a stronger development of the rational auxiliary function present in consciousness [and vice versa].[19]

The Two Attitude Types

According to Jung, his initial motivation for investigating typology was his need to understand why Freud's view of neurosis was so different from that of Adler.

Freud saw his patients as being preeminently dependent upon, and defining themselves in relation to, significant objects, particularly the parents. Adler's emphasis was on how a person, or subject, seeks his own security and supremacy. The one supposes that human behavior is conditioned by the object, the other finds the determining agency in the subject. Jung expressed appreciation for both points of view:

---

[19] *Psychological Types,* CW 6, par. 670.

The Freudian theory is attractively simple, so much so that it almost pains one if anybody drives in the wedge of a contrary assertion. But the same is true of Adler's theory. It too is of illuminating simplicity and explains as much as the Freudian theory. . . . But how comes it that each investigator sees only one side, and why does each maintain that he has the only valid view? . . . Both are obviously working with the same material; but because of personal peculiarities they each see things from a different angle.[20]

Jung concluded that these "personal peculiarities" were in fact due to typological differences: Freud's system was predominantly extraverted, while Adler's was introverted.[21]

These fundamentally opposite attitude types are found in both sexes and at all levels of society. They are not a matter of conscious choice or inheritance or education. Their occurrence is a general phenomenon having an apparently random distribution.

Two children in the same family may even be of opposite types. "Ultimately," writes Jung, "it must be the individual disposition which decides whether [one] will belong to this or that type."[22] In fact, he believed the type antithesis was due to some unconscious, instinctive cause, for which there was likely a biological foundation:

There are in nature two fundamentally different modes of adaptation which ensure the continued existence of the living organism. The one consists in a high rate of fertility, with low powers of defence and short duration of life for the single individual; the other consists in equipping the individual with numerous means of self-preservation plus a

---

[20] *Two Essays,* CW 7, pars. 56f.

[21] Von Franz distinguishes between Freud's psychological system and his personal typology. Freud himself, she believes, was an introverted feeling type, "and therefore his writings bear the characteristics of his inferior extraverted thinking." *(Jung's Typology,* p. 49)

[22] *Psychological Types,* CW 6, par. 560.

low fertility rate. . . . [Similarly] the peculiar nature of the extravert constantly urges him to expend and propagate himself in every way, while the tendency of the introvert is to defend himself against all demands from outside, to conserve his energy by withdrawing it from objects, thereby consolidating his own position.[23]

While it is apparent that some individuals have a greater capacity, or disposition, to adapt to life in one way or another, it is not known why. Jung suspected there might be physiological causes of which we have as yet no precise knowledge, since a reversal or distortion of type often proves harmful to one's physical well-being.

No one, of course, is only introverted or extraverted. Although each of us, in the process of following our dominant inclination or adapting to our immediate world, invariably develops one attitude more than the other, the opposite attitude is still potentially there.

Indeed, familial circumstances may force one at an early age to take on an attitude that is not natural, thus violating the individual's innate disposition. "As a rule," writes Jung, "whenever such a falsification of type takes place . . . the individual becomes neurotic later, and can be cured only by developing the attitude consonant with his nature."[24]

This certainly complicates the type issue, since everyone is more or less neurotic—that is, one-sided.

In general, the introvert is simply unconscious of his or her extraverted side, because of an habitual orientation toward the inner world. The extravert's introversion is similarly dormant, waiting to emerge.

In fact, the undeveloped attitude becomes an aspect of the shadow, all those things about ourselves we are not conscious

---

[23] Ibid., par. 559.
[24] Ibid., par. 560.

of, our unrealized potential, our "unlived life" (see below, "Typology and the Shadow," chapter 4). Moreover, being unconscious, when the inferior attitude surfaces—that is, when the introvert's extraversion, or the extravert's introversion, is constellated (activated)—it will tend to do so, just like the inferior function, in an emotional, socially unadapted way.

Since what is of value to the introvert is the opposite of what is important to the extravert, the inferior attitude regularly bedevils one's relationships with others.

To illustrate this, Jung tells the story of two youths, one an introverted type, the other extraverted, rambling in the countryside.[25] They come upon a castle. Both want to visit it, but for different reasons. The introvert wonders what it's like inside; the extravert is game for adventure.

At the gate the introvert draws back. "Perhaps we aren't allowed in," he says—imagining guard dogs, policemen and fines in the background. The extravert is undeterred. "Oh, they'll let us in all right," he says—with visions of kindly old watchmen and the possibility of meeting an attractive girl.

On the strength of extraverted optimism, the two finally get inside the castle. There they find some dusty rooms with a collection of old manuscripts. As it happens, old manuscripts are the main interest of the introvert. He whoops with joy and enthusiastically peruses the treasures. He talks to the caretaker, asks for the curator, becomes quite animated; his shyness has vanished, objects have taken on a seductive glamor.

Meanwhile, the spirits of the extravert have fallen. He becomes glum, begins to yawn. There are no kindly watchmen, no pretty girls, just an old castle made into a museum. The manuscripts remind him of a library, library is associated with university, university with studies and examinations. He finds the whole thing incredibly boring.

---

[25] See *Two Essays,* CW 7, pars. 81ff.

"Isn't it marvellous," cries the introvert, "look at these!"— to which the extravert replies grumpily, "Nothing here for me, let's go." This annoys the introvert, who secretly swears never again to go rambling with an inconsiderate extravert. The latter is completely frustrated and now can think of nothing but that he'd rather be out of doors on a lovely spring day.

Jung points out that the two youths are wandering together in happy symbiosis until they come upon the castle. They enjoy a degree of harmony because they are collectively adapted to each other; the natural attitude of the one complements the natural attitude of the other.

The introvert is curious but hesitant; the extravert opens the door. But once inside, the types invert themselves: the former becomes fascinated by the object, the latter by his negative thoughts. The introvert now cannot be induced to go out and the extravert regrets ever setting foot in the castle.

What has happened? The introvert has become extraverted and the extravert introverted. But the opposite attitude of each manifests in a socially inferior way: the introvert, overpowered by the object, doesn't appreciate that his friend is bored; the extravert, disappointed in his expectations of romantic adventure, becomes moody and sullen, and doesn't care about his friend's excitement.

This is a simple example of the way in which the inferior attitude is autonomous. What we are not conscious of in ourselves is by definition beyond our control. When the undeveloped attitude is constellated, we are prey to all kinds of disruptive emotions—we are "complexed."

In the above story the two youths could be called shadow brothers. In relationships between men and women, the psychological dynamics are better understood through Jung's concept of the contrasexual archetypes: anima—a man's inner ideal image of a woman—and animus—a woman's inner ideal image of a man.[26]

In general, the extraverted man has an introverted anima, while the introverted woman has an extraverted animus, and vice versa. This picture can change through psychological work on oneself, but these inner images are commonly projected onto persons of the opposite sex, with the result that either attitude type is prone to marry its opposite. This is likely to happen because each type is unconsciously complementary to the other.

Recall that the introvert is inclined to be reflective, to think things out and consider carefully before acting. Shyness and a degree of distrust of objects results in hesitation and some difficulty in adapting to the external world. The extravert, on the other hand, being attracted to the outer world, is fascinated by new and unknown situations. As a general rule the extravert acts first and thinks afterward; action is swift and not subject to misgivings or hesitation.

"The two types," writes Jung, "therefore seem created for a symbiosis. The one takes care of reflection and the other sees to the initiative and practical action. When the two types marry they may effect an ideal union."[27]

Discussing such a typical situation, Jung points out that it is ideal only so long as the partners are occupied with their adaptation to "the manifold external needs of life":

> But when . . . external necessity no longer presses, then they have time to occupy themselves with one another. Hitherto they stood back to back and defended themselves against necessity. But now they turn face to face and look for understanding—only to discover that they have never understood one another. Each speaks a different language. Then the conflict between the two types begins. This

---

[26] See "The Syzygy: Anima and Animus," *Aion,* CW 9ii.

[27] *Two Essays,* CW 7, par. 80.

struggle is envenomed, brutal, full of mutual depreciation, even when conducted quietly and in the greatest intimacy. For the value of the one is the negation of value for the other.[28]

In the course of life, we are generally obliged to develop both introversion and extraversion to some extent. This is necessary not only in order to coexist with others, but also for the development of individual character. "We cannot in the long run," writes Jung," allow one part of our personality to be cared for symbiotically by another." Yet that is in effect what is happening when we rely on friends, relatives or lovers to carry our inferior attitude or function.

If the inferior attitude is not consciously allowed some expression in our lives, we are likely to become bored and boring, uninteresting to both ourselves and others. And since there is energy tied up with whatever in ourselves is unconscious, we will not have the zest for life that goes with a well-balanced personality.

It is important to realize that a person's activities are not always a reliable indication of the attitude type. The life of the party may indeed be an extravert, but not necessarily. Similarly, long periods of solitude do not automatically mean that one is an introvert. The party-goer may be an introvert living out his shadow; the solitaire may be an extravert who has simply run out of steam, or has been forced by circumstances to be alone. In other words, while a particular activity may be associated with introversion or extraversion, this does not so easily translate into the type one is.

The crucial factor in determining type, as opposed to simply which attitude is currently prominent, is therefore not what one does but rather the motivation for doing it—*the direction in which one's energy naturally, and usually, flows:* for the

---

[28] Ibid.

extravert the object is interesting and attractive, while the subject, or psychic reality, is more important to the introvert.

Whether one is predominantly introverted or extraverted, there are inescapable psychological implications due to the role of the unconscious. Some of these are noted in the next section and more specifically in the chapters describing the characteristics of each attitude type. For particular medical consequences, see appendix 1, "The Clinical Significance of Extraversion and Introversion."

The Role of the Unconscious

The great difficulty in diagnosing the types is due to the fact that the dominant conscious attitude is unconsciously compensated or balanced by its opposite.

Introversion or extraversion, as a typical attitude, indicates an essential bias that conditions one's whole psychic process. The habitual mode of reaction determines not only the style of behavior, but also the quality of subjective experience. Moreover, it determines what is required in terms of compensation by the unconscious. Since either attitude is by itself one-sided, there would be a complete loss of psychic balance if there were no compensation by an unconscious counterposition.

Hence alongside or behind the introvert's usual way of functioning there is an unconscious extraverted attitude that automatically compensates the one-sidedness of consciousness. Similarly, the one-sidedness of extraversion is balanced or modified by an unconscious introverted attitude.

Strictly speaking, there is no demonstrable "attitude of the unconscious," but only ways of functioning that are colored by unconsciousness. It is in this sense that one can speak of a compensating attitude in the unconscious.

As we have seen, generally only one of the four functions is differentiated enough to be freely manipulable by the conscious will. The others are wholly or partially unconscious, and the inferior function mostly so. Thus the conscious orientation of the thinking type is balanced by unconscious feeling, and vice versa, while sensation is compensated by intuition, and so on.

Jung speaks of a "numinal accent" that falls on either the object or the subject, depending on whether one is extraverted or introverted. This numinal accent also "selects" one or other of the four functions, whose differentiation is essentially an empirical consequence of typical differences in the functional attitude.[29] Thus one finds extraverted feeling in an introverted intellectual, introverted sensation in an extraverted intuitive, and so on.

An additional problem in establishing a person's typology is that unconscious, undifferentiated functions can color a personality to such an extent that an outside observer might easily mistake one type for another.

For instance, the rational types (thinking and feeling) will have relatively inferior irrational functions (sensation and intuition); what they consciously and intentionally do may accord with reason (from their own point of view), but what happens to them may well be characterized by infantile, primitive sensations and intuitions. As Jung points out,

> Since there are vast numbers of people whose lives consist more of what happens to them than of actions governed by rational intentions, [an onlooker], after observing them closely, might easily describe [thinking and feeling types] as irrational. And one has to admit that only too often a man's unconscious makes a far stronger impression on an observer than his consciousness does, and that his actions are of considerably more importance than his rational intentions.[30]

---

[29] *Psychological Types,* CW 6, pars. 982ff.
[30] Ibid., par. 602.

It can be as difficult to establish one's own type as that of another person, especially when people have already become bored with their primary function and dominant attitude. Von Franz comments:

> They very often assure you with absolute sincerity that they belong to the type opposite from what they really are. The extravert swears that he is deeply introverted, and vice versa. This comes from the fact that the inferior function subjectively feels itself to be the real one, it feels itself the more important, more genuine attitude. . . . It does no good, therefore, to think of what *matters* most when trying to discover one's type; rather ask: "What do I habitually *do* most?"[31]

In practice, it is often helpful to ask oneself: What is my greatest cross? From what do I suffer the most? Where is it in life that I always knock my head against the wall and feel foolish? The answers to such questions generally lead to the inferior attitude and function, which then, with some determination and a good deal of patience, may perhaps be brought to a degree of consciousness.

Caveat to the Reader

It will now be apparent that while there is a simple elegance and symmetry to Jung's model of typology, its use as a diagnostic tool, or even as a guide to self-understanding, is far from simple. Jung warns his readers accordingly:

> Although there are doubtless individuals whose type can be recognized at first glance, this is by no means always the case. As a rule, only careful observation and weighing of the evidence permit a sure classification. However simple and clear the fundamental principle of the [opposing atti-

---

[31] *Jung's Typology,* p. 16.

tudes and functions] may be, in actual reality they are complicated and hard to make out, because every individual is an exception to the rule.[32]

What follows in the next chapters is for the most part a distillation of Jung's writings on the subject, observations by Marie-Louise von Franz and my own experience.

The reader is well advised to bear in mind that the descriptions of the types, and indeed the model itself, are not written in stone. As Jung himself pointed out, "the classification of types according to introversion and extraversion and the four basic functions [is not] the only possible one."[33] He did believe, however, that his model was useful, a practical way to orient ourselves, psychologically, as completely as when we locate a place geographically by latitude and longitude:

> The four functions are somewhat like the four points of the compass; they are just as arbitrary and just as indispensable. Nothing prevents our shifting the cardinal points as many degrees as we like in one direction or the other, or giving them different names. It is merely a question of convention and intelligibility. But one thing I must confess: I would not for anything dispense with this compass on my psychological voyages of discovery.[34]

It must further be acknowledged that anything written here (as anywhere else) cannot escape being biased according to the typology of the writer.

Personally, as far as I can tell after some twenty-five years of mulling over my own psychology, I *could be* an introverted sensation type—at the moment. My thinking is on the whole a

---

[32] *Psychological Types,* CW 6, par. 895.

[33] Ibid., par. 914.

[34] Ibid., par. 958f.

good auxiliary function, my feeling is erratic and intuition is particularly hard to come by.

But I remember earlier years when I functioned quite differently—in high school, for instance, as a blatant thinking type, and at university extraverted enough to be president of the Students' Council. And other times when introverted feeling was certainly dominant. And then of course there were those periods when intuition served me quite well indeed. . . .

Regarding Jung's own typology, his scientific investigations and insights point to a dominant thinking function, with sensation and intuition as well-developed auxiliary functions. However, it is also evident, from his ability to evaluate what something or someone was worth to him, that his feeling function was not noticeably inferior.

As to whether Jung was introverted or extraverted, one feels on safer ground; only an introvert would say, as Jung does in the prologue to his autobiographical *Memories, Dreams, Reflections,*

> When no answer comes from within to the problems and complexities of life, they ultimately mean very little. Outward circumstances are no substitute for inner experience. Therefore my life has been singularly poor in outward happenings. I cannot tell much about them, for it would strike me as hollow and insubstantial. I can understand myself only in the light of inner happenings. It is these that make up the singularity of my life.[35]

—though it is true that a lapsed extravert might say much the same thing. . . .

Welcome, then, to the adventure that is Jung's model of psychological types.

---

[35] *Memories, Dreams, Reflections* (London: Fontana Library paperback, 1967), p. 19.

2

Extraversion and the Four Functions

The Extraverted Attitude

When one's conscious orientation is determined by objective reality, the given facts in the outside world, we can speak of an extraverted attitude. When this is habitual, we have an extraverted type.

> Extraversion is characterized by interest in the external object, responsiveness, and a ready acceptance of external happenings, a desire to influence and be influenced by events, a need to join in and get "with it," the capacity to endure bustle and noise of every kind, and actually find them enjoyable, constant attention to the surrounding world, the cultivation of friends and acquaintances, none too carefully selected, and finally by the great importance attached to the figure one cuts, and hence by a strong tendency to make a show of oneself. Accordingly, the extravert's philosophy of life and his ethics are as a rule of a highly collective nature with a strong streak of altruism, and his conscience is in large measure dependent on public opinion. . . . His religious convictions are determined, so to speak, by majority vote.[1]

In general, the extravert trusts what is received from the outside world, and is similarly disinclined to submit personal motives to critical examination.

> The actual subject [the extraverted person] is, so far as possible, shrouded in darkness. He hides it from himself

---

[1] *Psychological Types,* CW 6, par. 972.

under veils of unconsciousness. . . . He has no secrets he has not long since shared with others. Should something unmentionable nevertheless befall him, he prefers to forget it. Anything that might tarnish the parade of optimism and positivism is avoided. Whatever he thinks, intends, and does is displayed with conviction and warmth.[2]

According to Jung, the psychic life of this type is enacted outside, strictly in reaction to the environment:

He lives in and through others; all self-communings give him the creeps. Dangers lurk there which are better drowned out by noise. If he should ever have a "complex," he finds refuge in the social whirl and allows himself to be assured several times a day that everything is in order.[3]

Although these comments seem rather harsh and uncomplimentary, Jung ends his description of the extraverted type with a qualified appreciation: "Provided he is not too much of a busy-body, too pushing, and too superficial, he can be a distinctly useful member of the community."[4]

Jung believed that type differentiation begins very early, "so early that in some cases one must speak of it as innate":

The earliest sign of extraversion in a child is his quick adaptation to the environment, and the extraordinary attention he gives to objects and especially to the effect he has on them. Fear of objects is minimal; he lives and moves among them with confidence. . . . and can therefore play with them freely and learn through them. He likes to carry his enterprises to the extreme and exposes himself to risks. Everything unknown is alluring.[5]

---

2 Ibid., par. 973

3 Ibid., par. 974.

4 Ibid.

5 Ibid., par. 896.

Although everyone is unavoidably affected by objective data, the extravert's thoughts, decisions and behavior patterns are actually determined, not simply influenced, by objective conditions rather than subjective views.

The extravert naturally has personal views, but these are subordinated to conditions as they are found in the outer world. The inner life always takes second place to outer necessity. One's whole consciousness is oriented outward, because that is where the essential and decisive determinants come from. Interest and attention are focused on objective events, on things and on other people, usually those in the immediate environment. Jung gives some examples of this type:

> St. Augustine: "I would not believe the Gospel if the authority of the Catholic Church did not compel it." A dutiful daughter: "I could not allow myself to think anything that would be displeasing to my father." One man finds a piece of modern music beautiful because everybody else pretends it is beautiful. Another marries in order to please his parents but very much against his own interests. There are people who contrive to make themselves ridiculous in order to amuse others. . . . There are not a few who in everything they do or don't do have but one motive in mind: what will others think of them?[6]

Prevailing moral standards dictate the extravert's personal standpoint. If the mores change, the extravert adjusts his views and behavior patterns to match. His capacity and inclination to adjust, to fit in with existing external conditions, is both his strength and his limitation. His tendency is so outer-directed that in general he will not pay much attention even to his own body—until it breaks down. The body itself is not sufficiently objective or "outside" to merit attention, hence the

---

[6] Ibid., par. 892.

satisfaction of elementary needs indispensable to physical well-being is easily overlooked.

Not only the body suffers, but the psyche as well. The former becomes apparent in physical symptoms that even the extravert cannot ignore, the latter in aberrant moods and behavior patterns that may be obvious only to others.

Extraversion is an obvious asset in social situations, and in responding to external requirements. But a too extraverted attitude may unknowingly sacrifice the subject in order to fulfil what it sees as objective demands—the needs of others, for instance, or the many requirements of an expanding business.

"This is the extravert's danger," notes Jung. "He gets sucked into objects and completely loses himself in them. The resultant functional disorders, nervous or physical, have a compensatory value, as they force him into an involuntary self-restraint."[7]

The form of neurosis most likely to afflict the extravert is hysteria. This typically manifests as a pronounced identification with persons in the immediate environment and an adjustment to external conditions that amounts to imitation.

Hysterics will go to great lengths to be interesting to other people and to produce a good impression. They are noticeably suggestible, overly influenced by others and effusive storytellers to the point of fantastically distorting the truth.

Hysterical neurosis begins as an exaggeration of all the usual characteristics of extraversion, and then is complicated by compensatory reactions from the unconscious. These latter counteract the exaggerated extraversion through symptoms that force the individual to introvert. This in turn constellates the extravert's inferior introversion and produces another set of symptoms, the most typical being morbid fantasy activity and the fear of being alone.

---

[7] Ibid., par. 565.

The extravert's tendency is to sacrifice inner reality to outer circumstances. This is not a problem so long as the extraversion is not too extreme. But to the extent that it becomes necessary to compensate the inclination to one-sidedness, there will arise an unconscious exaggeration of the subjective factor, namely, a markedly self-centered tendency in the unconscious.

All those needs or desires that are stifled or repressed by the conscious attitude come in the back door, so to speak, in the form of primitive and infantile thoughts and emotions that center on oneself.

The extravert's adjustment to objective reality effectively prevents low-powered subjective impulses from reaching consciousness. The repressed impulses, however, do not thereby lose their energy; only since they are unconscious they will manifest in primitive and archaic ways. As more and more subjective needs are suppressed or ignored, the build-up of unconscious energy works to undermine the conscious attitude.

The danger here is that the extravert, so habitually—and apparently selflessly—attuned to the outside world and the needs of other people, may in fact become completely indifferent. Writes Jung:

> The more complete the conscious attitude of extraversion is, the more infantile and archaic the unconscious attitude will be. The egoism which characterizes the extravert's unconscious attitude goes far beyond mere childish selfishness; it verges on the ruthless and brutal.[8]

Whenever the unconscious becomes overactive, it comes to light in symptomatic form. The egoism, infantilism and primitivism, normally a healthy compensation and relatively harmless, in extreme cases spurs consciousness to absurd exaggeration aimed at further repression of the unconscious.

---

8 Ibid., par. 572.

The eventual blowup may take an objective form, as one's outer activities become thwarted or colored by subjective considerations.

Jung tells of a printer who worked his way up until after years of struggle he became the owner of a thriving business. As it expanded it tightened his hold on him. Finally it swallowed up all his other interests. Then, in unconscious compensation for his one-sidedness, childhood memories of his great delight in painting and drawing came to life. But instead of renewing this activity as a hobby that would nicely complement his business concerns, he incorporated it into his business by embellishing his products artistically. Since his taste was primitive and infantile, his business ended in ruins.[9]

The result can also, or instead, be of a subjective nature— a nervous breakdown. This is likely to happen when the influence of the unconscious finally paralyzes conscious action:

> The demands of the unconscious then force themselves imperiously on consciousness and bring about a disastrous split which shows itself in one of two ways: either the subject no longer knows what he really wants and nothing interests him, or he wants too much at once and has too many interests, but in impossible things. The suppression of infantile and primitive demands for cultural reasons easily leads to a neurosis or to the abuse of narcotics such as alcohol, morphine, cocaine, etc. In more extreme cases the split ends in suicide.[10]

In general, the compensating attitude of the unconscious works to maintain psychic equilibrium. Hence even the individual who is normally extraverted will at times function in an introverted way. As long as the extraverted attitude predominates, however, the most developed function will manifest in

---

[9] Ibid., par. 572.

[10] Ibid., par. 573.

an extraverted way, while the inferior functions will be more or less introverted.

> The superior function is always an expression of the conscious personality, of its aims, will, and general performance, whereas the less differentiated functions fall into the category of things that simply "happen" to one.[11]

A good example of this is the extraverted feeling type who normally enjoys a close rapport with other people, yet occasionally voices opinions or makes remarks that are noticeably tactless. He may offer condolences at a wedding and congratulations at a funeral. Such gaffes come from inferior thinking, the fourth function, which in this type is not under conscious control and therefore not well related to others.

The unconscious regularly manifests through the less differentiated functions, which in the extravert have a subjective coloring and egocentric bias. Moreover, as mentioned above in the introduction, the constant influx of unconscious contents into the conscious psychological process is such that it is often difficult for an observer to tell which functions belong to the conscious and which to the unconscious personality. As Jung points out, this is further confused by the observer's own psychology:

> Generally speaking, a judging observer [thinking or feeling type] will tend to seize on the conscious character, while a perceptive observer [sensation type or intuitive] will be more influenced by the unconscious character, since judgment is chiefly concerned with the conscious motivation of the psychic process, while perception registers the process itself.[12]

---

[11] Ibid., par. 575.

[12] Ibid., par. 576.

In deciding to which attitude the superior function belongs, therefore, one must closely observe which function is more or less completely under conscious control, and which functions have a haphazard or random character. The superior function—if there is one at all—is always more highly developed than the others, which invariably possess infantile and primitive traits. In addition, one must always be mindful of one's own typological predisposition, which inevitably colors all observations.

The Extraverted Thinking Type

When the life of an individual is mainly governed by reflection, so that action proceeds from intellectually considered motives, we can speak of a thinking type. When this way of functioning is combined with an orientation toward the outer world, we have an extraverted thinking type.

The thinking function has no necessary connection with intelligence or the quality of thought, it is simply a process. Thinking is taking place when one formulates a scientific concept, reflects on the daily news or adds up a restaurant bill. It is extraverted or introverted according to whether it is oriented to the object or the subject.

Extraverted thinking is conditioned by objective data transmitted by sense perceptions. As a rational or judging function, thinking presupposes a judgment. In order to make a judgment, extraverted thinking fastens on the criteria supplied by external conditions, that is, those that have been transmitted through tradition and education.

Extraverted thinking types are captivated by the object, as though without it they could not exist. Reflection, for them, revolves around outer conditions and circumstances. This can be as fruitful and creative as introverted thinking, but to those of a different typology may seem quite limiting.

This type will, by definition, be a man whose constant endeavor—in so far, of course, as he is a pure type—is to make all his activities dependent on intellectual conclusions, which in the last resort are always oriented by objective data, whether these be external facts or generally accepted ideas. This type of man elevates objective reality, or an objectively oriented intellectual formula, into the ruling principle not only for himself but for his whole environment.[13]

At their best, extraverted thinkers are statesmen, lawyers, practical scientists, respected academics, successful entrepreneurs. They are excellent at establishing order, whether on paper, in their everyday lives, or at a business meeting. With a good sense of facts, they bring clarity into emotional situations. They are assets on any committee; they know Robert's Rules of Order and when to apply them.

At worst, this type is a religious zealot, a political opportunist, a con man (or woman), a strict pedagogue who brooks no dissent.

According to Jung, the extreme extraverted thinking types subordinate both themselves and others to their "formula," a system of rules, ideals and principles that in the end becomes a rigid moral code. Their benchmarks are justice and truth, based on what they consider to be the purest conceivable formulation of objective reality. "Oughts" and "musts" are typically prominent aspects of their intellectual standpoint. Those around them must, for everyone's good, obey the "universal law":

If the formula is broad enough, this type may play a very useful role in social life as a reformer or public prosecutor or purifier of conscience, or as the propagator of important innovations. But the more rigid the formula, the more he

---

13 Ibid., par. 585.

develops into a martinet, a quibbler, and a prig, who would like to force himself and others into one mould.[14]

Due to the extraverted attitude, the activities and influence of this type are generally more appreciated at a distance. While family and friends are likely to experience the unfavorable effects of what at close quarters feels like tyranny, their ideals and lofty principles will often find a ready response in those with whom they are not personally involved.

The most pernicious effects of extraverted thinking are visited on the person who functions in this way, for where the basic parameters of one's existence are objective ideas, ideals, rules and principles, little attention is paid to the subject.

> The fact that an intellectual formula never has been and never will be devised which could embrace and express the manifold possibilities of life must lead to the inhibition or exclusion of other activities and ways of living that are just as important. . . . Sooner or later, depending on outer circumstances or inner disposition, the potentialities repressed by the intellectual attitude will make themselves felt by disturbing the conscious conduct of life. When the disturbance reaches a definite pitch, we speak of a neurosis.[15]

The function most antithetical to thinking is feeling. Hence in this type, as shown in the diagram opposite, introverted feeling will be decidedly inferior. This means that those activities dependent on feeling—aesthetic taste, artistic sense, cultivation of friends, time with family, love relationships and so on—are most apt to suffer. Marie-Louise von Franz describes introverted feeling as "very difficult to understand":

> A very good example of it is the Austrian poet, Rainer Maria Rilke. He once wrote . . . "I love you, but it's none of your business"! That is love for love's sake. Feeling is

---

[14] Ibid.

[15] Ibid., par. 587.

very strong, but it does not flow toward the object. It is rather like being in a state of love with oneself. Naturally this type of feeling is very much misunderstood, and such people are considered very cold. But they are not at all; the feeling is all within them.[16]

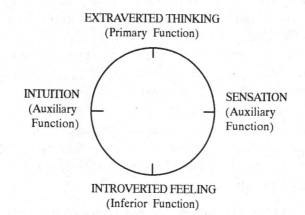

EXTRAVERTED THINKING
(Primary Function)

INTUITION
(Auxiliary
Function)

SENSATION
(Auxiliary
Function)

INTROVERTED FEELING
(Inferior Function)

To the extent that thinking is extraverted, the feeling function is infantile and repressed. "If the repression is successful," writes Jung,

the subliminal feeling then functions in a way that is opposed to the conscious aims, even producing effects whose cause is a complete enigma to the individual. For example, the conscious altruism of this type, which is often quite extraordinary, may be thwarted by a secret self-seeking which gives a selfish twist to actions that are in themselves disinterested. . . . There are extraverted idealists so consumed by their desire for the salvation of mankind that they will not shrink from any lie or trickery in pursuit of their ideal. . . . Their sanction is: the end justifies the means. Only an inferior function, operating unconsciously and in

---

[16] *Lectures on Jung's Typology* (Zurich: Spring Publications, 1971), p. 39.

secret, could seduce otherwise reputable men into such aberrations.[17]

Inferior introverted feeling typically manifests in a conscious attitude that is more or less impersonal. That is why this type may seem cold and unfriendly. From their point of view, however, they are simply more interested in the facts than in what effect their attitude may have on others.

In the extreme case, this leads to neglect of their own and their family's vital interests. In compensation, the unconscious feelings become highly personal and oversensitive—petty, aggressive and mistrustful of others.

Meanwhile, the espoused intellectual "formula," which may actually have intrinsic merit, becomes more rigid and dogmatic, completely closed to any modifications. It may even take on the religious quality of absoluteness.

> Now all the psychological tendencies it has repressed build up a counterposition in the unconscious and give rise to paroxysms of doubt. The more it tries to fend off the doubt, the more fanatical the conscious attitude becomes, for fanaticism is nothing but over-compensated doubt. This development ultimately leads to an exaggerated defence of the conscious position and to the formation of a counterposition in the unconscious absolutely opposed to it.[18]

At this point there is danger of a complete collapse of the conscious attitude. Unless the disturbing unconscious factors are brought into consciousness, the normally positive and creative thinking of the extravert becomes stagnant and regressive. The formula degenerates to an intellectual superstition, while the individual becomes a sullen, resentful pedant, or, in the extreme case, a misanthropic recluse.

---

[17] *Psychological Types,* CW 6, par. 588.
[18] Ibid., par. 591.

The inferior introverted feeling of this type also manifests in ways that are less unpleasant but, to the observer, no less puzzling: sudden and inexplicable outbursts of affection; fierce and lasting loyalties that are "unreasonable"; sentimental attachments or mystical interests that defy all logic.

In such instances, the conscious thinking process is subverted by primitive reactions that have their source in the subject's unconscious and undifferentiated feeling.

The Extraverted Feeling Type

The feeling of the extraverted type, like extraverted thinking, is oriented by objective data and generally in harmony with objective values.

As a rational function that determines what something is worth, one might assume that feeling would be based on subjective values. According to Jung, however, this is true only of introverted feeling:

> Extraverted feeling has detached itself as much as possible from the subjective factor and subordinated itself entirely to the influence of the object. Even when it appears not to be qualified by a concrete object, it is none the less still under the the spell of traditional or generally accepted values of some kind.[19]

It is characteristic of extraverted feeling that it seeks to create or maintain harmonious conditions in the surrounding environment. For instance, the extraverted feeling type will praise something as "beautiful" or "good" not because of a subjective evaluation, but because it is proper to do so according to the social situation. This is not pretence or hypocrisy, but a genuine expression of feeling in its extraverted mode—an act of adjustment to objective criteria.

---

[19] Ibid., par. 595.

> A painting, for instance, is called "beautiful" because a painting hung in a drawing room and bearing a well-known signature is generally assumed to be beautiful, or because to call it "hideous" would presumably offend the family or its fortunate possessor, or because the visitor wants to create a pleasant feeling atmosphere, for which purpose everything must be felt as agreeable.[20]

Without extraverted feeling, a "civilized" social life would be virtually impossible. Collective expressions of culture depend on it. Out of extraverted feeling people go to the theater, to concerts, to church and the opera; they take part in business conventions, company picnics, birthday parties, etc.; send Christmas and Easter cards, attend weddings and funerals, celebrate anniversaries and take notice of Mother's Day.

Extraverted feeling types are generally amiable and make friends easily. They are quick to evaluate what the outer situation requires, and readily sacrifice themselves for others. They exude an atmosphere of warm acceptance, they get the ball rolling at a party. Except in extreme cases, the feeling has some personal quality—there is a genuine rapport with others—even though the subjective factor is largely suppressed. The predominant impression is of a person well adjusted to external conditions and social values.

Jung describes the typical manifestation of extraverted feeling in a woman:

> The "suitable" man is loved, and no one else; he is suitable not because he appeals to her hidden subjective nature—about which she usually knows nothing—but because he comes up to all reasonable expectations in the matter of age, position, income, size and respectability of his family, etc. . . . The love feeling of this type of woman . . . is genuine and not just shrewd. . . . There are countless "reasonable" marriages of this kind and they are by no

---

[20] Ibid.

means the worst. These women are good companions and excellent mothers so long as the husbands and children are blessed with the conventional psychic constitution.[21]

The danger for this type lies in being overwhelmed by the object—traditional and generally accepted standards—and so losing any semblance of subjective feeling, that is, what is going on in oneself.

Extraverted feeling that is devoid of personal parameters loses all its charm, and, as with extreme extraversion in general, is unconscious of ulterior, self-centered motives. It meets the demands or expectations that are presented by outer situations and stops there. It satisfies the required aesthetics of the moment, but it is sterile. The normally heart-felt expressions of feeling become mechanical, the empathetic gestures seem theatrical or calculating.

> If this process goes any further, a curiously contradictory dissociation of feeling results: everything becomes an object of feeling valuations, and innumerable relationships are entered into which are all at variance with each other. As this situation would become quite impossible if the subject received anything like due emphasis, even the last vestiges of a real personal standpoint are suppressed. The subject becomes so enmeshed in the network of individual feeling processes that to the observer it seems as though there were merely a feeling process and no longer a subject of feeling. Feeling in this state has lost all human warmth; it gives the impression of being put on, fickle, unreliable, and in the worst cases hysterical.[22]

For this type it is of the utmost importance to establish a good feeling rapport with the environment. But when this becomes too important, the subject—the person who feels—is

---

21 Ibid., par. 597.
22 Ibid., par. 596.

engulfed. Then feeling loses its personal quality and becomes feeling for its own sake. The personality itself is dissolved in a succession of momentary feeling states, often in conflict with each other. To the observer, this appears as different moods and statements that are blatantly contradictory.

Indeed, thinking, the other rational function, is invariably repressed when feeling is dominant. Nothing disturbs feeling more than thinking (and, as we have seen, vice versa). Feeling types do not have to think about what someone or something is worth to them, they just *know.*

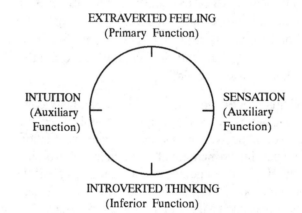

EXTRAVERTED FEELING
(Primary Function)

INTUITION
(Auxiliary
Function)

SENSATION
(Auxiliary
Function)

INTROVERTED THINKING
(Inferior Function)

The extraverted feeling type may think a great deal, and in fact be quite clever, but thinking is always subordinated to feeling. Hence logical conclusions, processes of thought that might lead to a disturbance of feeling, are rejected out of hand. "Everything that fits in with objective values," writes Jung, "is good, and is loved, and everything else seems to . . . exist in a world apart."[23]

In the extreme case, the healthy compensatory attitude of the unconscious becomes open opposition. This appears first

---

[23] Ibid., par. 598.

in extravagant displays of feeling—gushing talk, passionate declarations, etc.—that seem intended to block out logical conclusions that are incompatible with the feeling "required" at the moment.

> Though the thinking of the extraverted feeling type is repressed as an independent function, the repression is not complete . . . . It is suffered to exist as a servant of feeling, or rather as its slave. . . . Accordingly the unconscious of this type contains first and foremost a peculiar kind of thinking, a thinking that is infantile, archaic, negative. So long as the conscious feeling preserves its personal quality, or, to put it another way, so long as the personality is not swallowed up in successive states of feeling, this unconscious thinking remains compensatory.[24]

When the personality dissolves into a succession of contradictory feeling states, however, the ego identity is lost and the subject falls into the unconscious. The stronger the conscious feeling, the stronger becomes the unconscious opposition. "The 'nothing but' type of thinking comes into its own here," writes Jung, "since it effectively depotentiates all feelings that are bound to the object."[25]

People of this type have at times the most negative and deprecatory thoughts about the very persons most valued by their feelings. Indeed, the presence of such thinking, normally dormant in the background, is one of the main indications that extraverted feeling is the dominant function.

Von Franz points out that such thoughts are typically based on a very cynical outlook on life; moreover, they are usually turned inward:

> At bottom he allows himself to think that he is a nobody, that his life is worthless, and that everybody else might de-

---

[24] Ibid., par. 600.
[25] Ibid.

velop and get on the path of individuation, but he is hopeless. These thoughts dwell in the back of his mind and from time to time, when he is depressed or not well off, or especially when he introverts, that is when he is alone for half a minute, this negative thing whispers at the back of his head: "You are nothing, everything about you is wrong."[26]

As a result, the extraverted feeling type hates to be alone; when such negative thoughts start to come up, the usual reaction is to turn on the television or rush out to meet a friend.

The Extraverted Sensation Type

Extraverted sensation is preeminently oriented to objective reality. As a way of perceiving through the physical senses, the sensation function, whether introverted or extraverted, is naturally dependent on objects. But, as we will see with introverted sensation, it is also possible to be subjectively oriented toward what is objectively perceived.

In extraverted sensation, the subjective component is inhibited or repressed. The response to the object is conditioned *by* the object. When this is an individual's habitual way of functioning, we have an extraverted sensation type.

This type will seek out those objects, both people and situations, that excite the strongest sensations. The result is a strong sensuous tie to the outside world.

> Objects are valued in so far as they excite sensations, and, so far as lies within the power of sensation, they are fully accepted into consciousness whether they are compatible with rational judgments or not. The sole criterion of their value is the intensity of the sensation produced by their objective qualities. . . . However, it is only concrete, sensu-

---

[26] *Jung's Typology,* p. 45.

ously perceived objects or processes that excite sensations for the extravert; those, exclusively, which everyone everywhere would sense as concrete. Hence the orientation of such an individual accords with purely sensuous reality.[27]

Although such people have little patience for, or understanding of, abstract reality, their sense for objective facts is extremely well developed. They are masters at the details of life. They can read maps, find their way around a strange city; their rooms are neat and tidy; they don't forget appointments and they are punctual; they don't lose keys; they remember to turn the stove off and don't leave the lights on overnight. They are found among engineers, editors, athletes and people in business.

Extraverted sensation types pay attention to the externals of life. They are fashion conscious and like to be impeccably dressed; they keep a good table with plenty of fine wine; they surround themselves with exquisite possessions, beautiful people. They love parties and active sports, meetings and committees. They are the kind of persons who climb Mount Everest "because it's there." Those who do not share their typological predilections are dubbed as stuffy and timid.

In short, this type is oriented toward concrete enjoyment —"real life," lived to the full.

> To feel the object, to have sensations and if possible enjoy them—that is his constant aim. He is by no means unlovable; on the contrary, his lively capacity for enjoyment makes him very good company; he is usually a jolly fellow, and sometimes a refined aesthete. . . . Conjectures that go beyond the concrete are admitted only on condition that they enhance sensation. The intensification does not necessarily have to be pleasurable, for this type need not be a common voluptuary; he is merely desirous of the

---

[27] *Psychological Types,* CW 6, par. 605.

strongest sensations, and these, by his very nature, he can receive only from outside.[28]

The ideal of extraverted sensation types is to be well adjusted to reality, things as they are—as *they* see and experience them. Their love is irrevocably dependent on the physical attractions of the loved one. What their partner thinks, feels or wonders about may be of little or no interest—but they will notice and remark on details other types are oblivious to: the brand of after-shave, the style of earrings, new hair-do, the cut of a suit or dress. They may also be excellent lovers, since their sense of touch is naturally attuned to the other's body.

EXTRAVERTED SENSATION
(Primary Function)

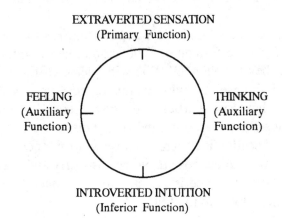

FEELING
(Auxiliary
Function)

THINKING
(Auxiliary
Function)

INTROVERTED INTUITION
(Inferior Function)

The Achilles heel of this type is introverted intuition. What is not factual, what cannot be seen, heard, touched or smelled is automatically suspect. Anything that comes from inside seems morbid. Only in the realm of tangible reality can they breathe freely. Their thoughts and feelings will be explained by objective causes or the influence of others. A change in mood is unhesitatingly blamed on the weather. Psychic conflicts are unreal—"nothing but" imagination—an unhealthy

[28] Ibid., par. 607.

state of affairs that will soon clear up when surrounded by friends.

Within the subject, inferior intuition manifests in negative premonitions, suspicious thoughts, possibilities of disaster, dark fantasies, etc. Von Franz says inferior intuition is "like a dog sniffing in garbage pails."[29]

The most disagreeable traits of this type emerge to the extent that the pursuit of sensation becomes all-consuming. In the extreme case, they become crude pleasure-seekers, unscrupulous aesthetes, gross hedonists. Jung describes what this looks like in a man:

> Although the object [is] quite indispensable to him, yet, as something existing in its own right, it is none the less devalued. It is ruthlessly exploited and squeezed dry, since now its sole use is to stimulate sensation. The bondage to the object is carried to the extreme limit. In consequence, the unconscious is forced out of its compensatory role into open opposition. Above all, repressed intuitions begin to assert themselves in the form of projections.[30]

Projection here gives rise to the wildest suspicions, jealous fantasies and anxiety states, especially if sexuality is involved. These have their source in the repressed inferior functions and are all the more remarkable since they typically rest on the most absurd assumptions, in complete contrast to the extraverted sensation type's conscious sense of reality and normally easy-going attitude.

> More acute cases develop every sort of phobia, and, in particular, compulsion symptoms. The pathological contents have a markedly unreal character, with a frequent moral or religious streak . . . or a grotesquely punctilious morality combined with primitive, "magical" superstitions

---

29 *Jung's Typology,* p. 24.

30 *Psychological Types,* CW 6, par. 608.

that fall back on abstruse rights. . . . The whole structure of
thought and feeling seems . . . to be twisted into a pathological parody: reason turns into hair-splitting pedantry,
morality into dreamy moralizing and blatant Pharisaism,
religion into ridiculous superstition, and intuition, the no-
blest gift of man, into meddlesome officiousness, poking
into every corner; instead of gazing into the far distance, it
descends to the lowest level of human meanness.[31]

As with any of the functions that attain an abnormal degree of
one-sidedness, therefore, there is always the danger that
consciousness will be overpowered by the unconscious.

Only occasionally, of course, does the psychological
situation become pathological. More usually, the compensating
inferior function simply imparts a rather charming air of
inconsistency to the personality. In this type, for instance,
introverted intuition is seen in a naive attachment to religious
movements, a childish interest in the occult or sudden spiritual
insights.

The Extraverted Intuitive Type

Intuition is the function of unconscious perception. In the
extraverted attitude, intuition is directed to, and conditioned
by, external objects. When this way of functioning predominates, we can speak of an extraverted intuitive type. Jung
writes:

> The intuitive function is represented in consciousness by an
> attitude of expectancy, by vision and penetration; but only
> from the subsequent result can it be established how much
> of what was "seen" was actually in the object, and how

---

[31] Ibid., pars. 608ff.

much was "read into" it. Just as sensation, when it is the dominant function, is not a mere reactive process of no further significance for the object, but an activity that seizes and shapes its object, so intuition is not mere perception, or vision, but an active, creative process that puts into the object just as much as it takes out. Since it does this unconsciously, it also has an unconscious effect on the object.[32]

The primary purpose of intuition is to perceive aspects of the world that are not apprehended by the other functions. Intuition is like a sixth sense that "sees" something not actually there. Intuitive thoughts come out of the blue, so to speak, as a hunch or a guess.

In the extravert, where intuition is oriented toward things and other people, there is an extraordinary ability to sense what is going on behind the scenes, under the surface; it "sees through" the outer layer. Where the comparatively mundane perception of the sensation type sees "a thing" or "a person," the intuitive sees its soul.

When intuition is dominant, thinking and feeling will be more or less repressed, while sensation—the other irrational function, but attuned to physical reality—is most inaccessible to consciousness.

Sensation is a hindrance to clear, unbiased, naive perception; its intrusive sensory stimuli direct attention to the physical surface, to the very things round and beyond which intuition tries to peer. . . . [The intuitive] does have sensations, of course, but he is not guided by them as such; he uses them merely as starting-points for his perceptions. He selects them by conscious predilection.[33]

---

[32] Ibid., par. 610.

[33] Ibid., par. 611.

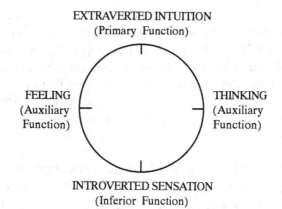

EXTRAVERTED INTUITION
(Primary Function)

FEELING
(Auxiliary
Function)

THINKING
(Auxiliary
Function)

INTROVERTED SENSATION
(Inferior Function)

Where extraverted sensation seeks the highest pitch of physical realism, extraverted intuition strives to apprehend the widest range of possibilities inherent in the objective situation. To the former, an object is simply an object; the latter goes right past its outer appearance and fastens on what could be done with it, how it might be used.

A businessman who was a sensation type asked a friend, an intuitive artist, to design a logo for his new business. The company was called Belltower Enterprises. The artist came up with the following design:

"What's that?" said the sensation type, genuinely puzzled. He saw only three ovals connected by dotted lines. "Don't you see," explained the intuitive, "the dotted line shows how the clapper moves when the bell tolls."

The difference between the two is equally striking when they enter an empty house. The sensation type sees the bare walls, the shabby window casements, the dirty floors. The intuitive sees rather what can be done with the space—the walls painted in soft pastels, pictures in place, sanded and shiny floors, clean windows and curtains, even where the furniture will go.

Sensation types see only what is in front of them. Intuitives see the same scene transformed, as if in an inner vision, as if the house were already furnished and completely redecorated. None of this is available to the sensation function, which sees merely what is there at that moment in time. Hence the sensation type is well advised to bring along an intuitive when shopping for a house. Naturally, the opposite is also true, for while the intuitive is spellbound by the possibilities, the sensation type notices whether damp is seeping into the basement, the state of the plumbing, the number of electrical plugs, the distance to the nearest school, and so on.

Extraverted intuition is constantly on the lookout for new opportunities, new fields to conquer. Existing situations are not interesting for long; the intuitive is quickly bored by "things as they are." Intuition can ferret out possibilities, but to actualize them requires the focusing abilities of sensation and thinking.

> Because extraverted intuition is oriented by the object, there is a marked dependence on external situations, but it is altogether different from the dependence of the sensation type. The intuitive is never to be found in the world of accepted reality-values, but he has a keen nose for anything new and in the making. Because he is always seeking out new possibilities, stable conditions suffocate him. . . . So long as a new possibility is in the offing, the intuitive is bound to it with the shackles of fate.[34]

The main dilemma for extraverted intuitives is that the very situations that seem to promise freedom or excitement quickly

---

[34] Ibid., par. 613.

lead, once their possibilities have been exhausted, to the feeling of being imprisoned. It is hard to stick to something for any length of time. As soon as no further developments can be divined, they will leave and seek something new.

Characteristically, there is a noticeable lack of judgment, for good judgment comes from a well-developed thinking or feeling function. But extreme intuitives are not influenced by thoughts or feelings, neither their own nor those of others. To the extent that their vision is all-important, to everything else they are indifferent. Others may see them as callous and exploitative, whereas they are simply being too one-sidedly true to their type.

Such people are nevertheless indispensable in the areas of culture and economics. Their peculiar talents suit them well for professions where the ability to see possibilities in external situations is of great value. They are found among captains of industry, innovative entrepreneurs, speculative stockbrokers, visionary statesmen, etc. In the social sphere, they have an uncanny ability to make the "right" connections.

When this type's orientation is more to people than to things, they show an exceptional ability to diagnose potential capabilities. Hence they often bring out the best in others, and can be uncanny matchmakers. They are also the natural champions of minorities (those with a future) and have an unrivaled capacity for kindling enthusiasm for anything new—though they themselves may be indifferent to it the next day.

The extraverted intuitive who fastens on the work of creative artists is psychologically well suited to seeing its commercial possibilities and doing something about it. Von Franz comments:

> Creative people themselves are introverted and are so occupied with their creations that they cannot attend to the bringing out of their work. The work itself takes up so much of their energy that they cannot be bothered with how it should be presented to the world, how to advertise it, or

anything of that kind. . . . Very often, then, the extraverted intuitive comes along and helps. But, naturally, if he does that all his life, he begins projecting a minor creative ability of his own onto the artist, and so he loses himself. Sooner or later such people have to . . . attend to their own inferior sensation and to what might come out of it.[35]

This is the great danger for extraverted intuitives, that they will spend their time and energy on possibilities, particularly those of others, and never realize anything themselves. They can't stay put; they start things but can't sustain the interest to finish them. For this reason they are often seen as frivolous or carefree adventurers. They have a vision of what could be, but can't be bothered to implement it. Typically, they get a business off the ground and leave it on the brink of success; hence others often reap where they have sown.

The more extreme this type is—the more one's ego becomes identified with all the visionary possibilities—then the more active becomes the unconscious in terms of compensation.

The unconscious of the intuitive bears some resemblance to that of the sensation type. Thinking and feeling, being largely repressed, come up with infantile, archaic thoughts and feelings similar to those of the countertype. They take the form of intense projections which are just as absurd as [those of the sensation type], though they seem to lack the "magical" character of the latter and are chiefly concerned with quasi-realities such as sexual suspicions, financial hazards, forebodings of illness, etc.[36]

Other pathological symptoms in this type include neurotic phobias and an unconscious, compulsive tie to the sensation

---

[35] *Jung's Typology,* p. 31.
[36] *Psychological Types,* CW 6, par. 615.

aroused by the object, whether that be another person or material possessions.

In addition, since introverted sensation is here the most inferior function, there is usually a marked split between consciousness and the personal body. Even "normal" extraverted intuitives tend to pay little attention to their physical needs. They simply do not notice, for instance, when they are tired or hungry. This neglect of the subject will eventually take its toll in all manner of physical illness, both real and imaginary.

A more usual, and relatively harmless, manifestation of this type's compensating inferior function is seen in an exaggerated attention to the body, personal hygiene, fitness fads, health foods, etc.

3

Introversion and the Four Functions

The Introverted Attitude

The distinguishing feature of introversion, as opposed to extraversion, is that whereas the latter relates primarily to the object and data originating in the outside world, introversion finds its orientation in inner, personal factors.

> A person of this type might say: "I know I could give my father the greatest pleasure if I did so and so, but I don't happen to think that way." Or: "I see that the weather has turned out bad, but in spite of it I shall carry out my plan." This type does not travel for pleasure but to execute a preconceived idea. . . . At every step the sanction of the subject must be obtained, and without it nothing can be undertaken or carried out. Such people would have replied to St. Augustine [see above, p. 39]: "I would believe the Gospel if the authority of the Catholic Church did *not* compel it." Always he has to prove that everything he does rests on his own decisions and convictions, and never because he is influenced by anyone, or desires to please or conciliate some person or opinion.[1]

Naturally, an introverted consciousness can be well aware of external conditions, but subjective determinants are decisive as the motivating force. While the extravert responds to what comes to the subject from the object (outer reality), the introvert relates mainly to the impressions aroused by the object in the subject (inner reality).

---

[1] *Psychological Types,* CW 6, par. 893.

Jung is characteristically blunt in describing the traits of this type:

> The introvert is not forthcoming, he is as though in continual retreat before the object. He holds aloof from external happenings, does not join in, has a distinct dislike of society as soon as he finds himself among too many people. In a large gathering he feels lonely and lost. The more crowded it is, the greater becomes his resistance. He is not in the least "with it," and has no love of enthusiastic get-togethers. He is not a good mixer. What he does, he does in his own way, barricading himself against influences from outside. . . . He is easily mistrustful, self-willed, often suffers from inferiority feelings and for this reason is also envious. He confronts the world with an elaborate defensive system compounded of scrupulosity, pedantry, frugality, cautiousness, painful conscientiousness, stiff-lipped rectitude, politeness, and open-eyed distrust. . . . Under normal conditions he is pessimistic and worried, because the world and human beings are not in the least good but crush him. . . .
>
> His own world is a safe harbour, a carefully tended and walled-in garden, closed to the public and hidden from prying eyes. His own company is the best.[2]

No wonder the introverted attitude is often seen as auto-erotic, egocentric, egotistical, even pathological. But in Jung's opinion, this simply reflects the normal bias of the extraverted attitude, which is by definition convinced of the superiority of the object.

> We must not forget—although the extravert is only too prone to do so—that perception and cognition are not purely objective, but are also subjectively conditioned. The world exists not merely in itself, but also as it appears to

---

2 Ibid., pars. 976f.

me. . . . By overvaluing our capacity for objective cognition we repress the importance of the subjective factor.[3]

By the "subjective factor," Jung understands "that psychological action or reaction which merges with the effect produced by the object and so gives rise to a new psychic datum."[4] For example, it used to be thought that the so-called scientific method was completely objective, but it is now acknowledged that the observation and interpretation of any kind of data is colored by the subjective attitude of the observer, which necessarily involves both one's expectations and one's psychological predisposition.[5]

Jung points out that our knowledge of the past depends on the subjective reactions of those who experienced and described what was happening around them.[6] In this sense, subjectivity is a reality as firmly based in tradition and experience as is orientation toward the objective world. In other words, introversion is no less "normal" than extraversion.

Both, of course, are relative. Where the extravert sees the introvert as unsociable, unable or unwilling to adapt to the "real" world, the introvert judges the extravert as shallow, lacking in inner depth. There is as much and as little justification for the one attitude as for the other, since each has its strengths and its weaknesses.

One of the signs of introversion in a child, Jung notes, "is a reflective, thoughtful manner, marked shyness and even fear of unknown objects":

Very early there appears a tendency to assert himself over familiar objects, and attempts are made to master them.

---

[3] Ibid., par. 621.

[4] Ibid., par. 622.

[5] See, for instance, Fritjof Capra, *The Tao of Physics* (New York: Bantam Books, 1984).

[6] *Psychological Types,* CW 6, par. 622.

Everything unknown is regarded with mistrust; outside influences are usually met with violent resistance. The child wants his own way, and under no circumstances will he submit to an alien rule he cannot understand. When he asks questions, it is not from curiosity or a desire to create a sensation, but because he wants names, meanings, explanations to give him subjective protection against the object. I have seen an introverted child who made his first attempts to walk only after he had learned the names of all the objects in the room he might touch.[7]

This kind of apotropaic action—a "magical" depotentiation of the object—is also characteristic of the introverted attitude in the adult. There is a marked tendency to devalue things and other persons, to deny their importance. Just as the object plays too great a role in the extraverted attitude, it has too little meaning for the introvert.

To the extent that consciousness is subjectivized and excessive importance is attached to the ego, there naturally arises, by way of compensation, an unconscious reinforcement of the object's influence. This makes itself felt, writes Jung, "as an absolute and irrepressible tie to the object":

The more the ego struggles to preserve its independence, freedom from obligation, and superiority, the more it becomes enslaved to the objective data. The individual's freedom of mind is fettered by the ignominy of his financial dependence, his freedom of action trembles in the face of public opinion, his moral superiority collapses in a morass of inferior relationships, and his desire to dominate ends in a pitiful craving to be loved. It is now the unconscious that takes care of the relation to the object, and it does so in a way that is calculated to bring the illusion of power and the fantasy of superiority to utter ruin.[8]

---

[7] Ibid., par. 897.

[8] Ibid., par. 626.

A person in this psychological situation can wear himself out with defence measures (in order to preserve the illusion of superiority), while making fruitless attempts to assert himself —impose his will on the object. "He is terrified of strong affects in others," writes Jung, "and is hardly ever free from the dread of falling under hostile influences."[9]

Naturally this takes a great deal of energy. A tremendous inner struggle is needed all the time in order to keep going. Thus the introvert is particularly prone to psychasthenia, "a malady," notes Jung, "characterized on the one hand by extreme sensitivity and on the other by great proneness to exhaustion and chronic fatigue."[10]

In less extreme cases, introverts are simply more conservative than not: they husband their energy and would rather stay put than run about. But due to the habitual subjective orientation, there may also be a noticeable degree of ego inflation, coupled with an unconscious power drive.

Although Jung recognized the "peculiarities" of the introvert, especially as judged by the extraverted attitude, he also pointed out that the introvert "is by no means a social loss. His retreat into himself is not a final renunciation of the world, but a search for quietude, where alone it is possible for him to make his contribution to the life of the community."[11]

In addition, whereas the extravert tends to avoid introspection, "self-communings," writes Jung, are a pleasure for the introvert:

> He feels at home in his world, where the only changes are made by himself. His best work is done with his own resources, on his own initiative, and in his own way. If ever he succeeds, after long and often wearisome struggles, in

---

9 Ibid., par. 627.

10 Ibid., par. 626.

11 Ibid., par. 979.

assimilating something alien to himself, he is capable of turning it to excellent account.[12]

The Introverted Thinking Type

Thinking in the introverted attitude is oriented primarily by the subjective factor. Whether the thinking process focuses on concrete or abstract objects, its motivation comes from within.

Introverted thinking depends on neither immediate experience nor generally accepted, traditional ideas. It is no less (or more) logical than extraverted thinking, but it is neither motivated by objective reality nor directed toward it.

> External facts [writes Jung] are not the aim and origin of this thinking, though the introvert would often like to make his thinking appear so. It begins with the subject and leads back to the subject, far though it may range into the realm of actual reality. . . . It formulates questions and creates theories, it opens up new prospects and insights, but with regard to facts its attitude is one of reserve. . . . What seems to it of paramount importance is the development and presentation of the subjective idea, of the initial symbolic image hovering darkly before the mind's eye.[13]

In other words, where extraverted thinking seeks to get the facts straight and then think about them, introverted thinking is concerned with the clarification of ideas, or even the mentation process itself, and only then (perhaps) with their practical application. Both excel at bringing order into life; one works from the outside in, the other from the inside out.

Introverted thinkers, being by definition not so practical minded, tend to be theoreticians. Intensity is their aim, not

---

12 Ibid., par. 977.
13 Ibid., par. 628.

extensity. They follow their ideas inward, not outward. Von Franz describes them as follows:

> In science these are the people who are perpetually trying to prevent their colleagues from getting lost in experiments and who, from time to time, try to get back to basic concepts and ask what we are really doing mentally. In physics, there is generally one professor for practical physics and another for theoretical physics: one lectures on the Wilson Chamber and the building up of experiments, the other on mathematical principles and the theory of science.[14]

Like extraverted thinking types, introverted thinkers make good editors, though they may fuss endlessly over just the right word. Since their thought process is logical and straightforward, they are especially good at filling in the gaps in the so-called nonlinear or lateral thinking—the leaping from thought to thought—that distinguishes the intuitive. As writers, their forte is not originality of content but rather clarity and precision in the organization and presentation of the available material.

Lacking an orientation to outer facts, introverted thinking types easily get lost in a fantasy world. Their subjective orientation may seduce them into creating theories for their own sake, apparently based on reality, but actually tied to an inner image. In the extreme case this image becomes all-consuming and alienates them from others.

As might be expected, these types tend to be indifferent to the opinions of others. To the extent that they are not influenced, neither do they try to influence. They will present their logical assessment of reality—as they see it—and not care one way or another how it is received.

---

[14] *Lectures on Jung's Typology* (Zurich: Spring Publications, 1971), p. 41.

The particularly weak point of this type, the inferior function, is extraverted feeling. Bound up with an inner world of thoughts and ideals, one is apt to be oblivious to the objective requirements of, say, a relationship. It isn't that such persons don't love, but they are simply at a loss to know how to express it. Their feelings tend to be whimsical—they often don't know how they feel at all—but when they surface, usually contaminated with affect, they can be overwhelming and uncontrollable. (It is at such times that it becomes imperative to distinguish between emotional reactions and feeling as a psychological function.)

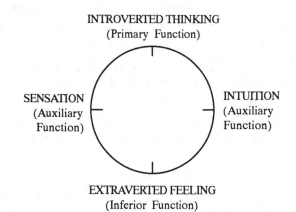

INTROVERTED THINKING
(Primary Function)

SENSATION
(Auxiliary
Function)

INTUITION
(Auxiliary
Function)

EXTRAVERTED FEELING
(Inferior Function)

Such unconscious feeling can be a delightful surprise, but also quite burdensome when it is directed toward another person. Von Franz (a self-confessed introverted thinking type) says that inferior extraverted feeling manifests as a kind of "sticky attachment":

> While the extraverted thinking type deeply loves his wife but says with Rilke [see above, p. 46]: "I love you, but it is none of your business," the feeling of the introverted thinking type is tied to external objects. He would therefore say, in the Rilke style, "I love you, and it will be your business; I'll make it your business!" . . . The inferior

feeling of both types is sticky, and the extraverted thinking type has that kind of invisible faithfulness which can last endlessly. The same is true for the extraverted feeling of the introverted thinking type, except that it will not be invisible. . . . It resembles the glue-like flow of feeling in an epileptoid person; it has that kind of sticky, dog-like attachment which, especially to the beloved, is not amusing. You could compare the inferior feeling of an introverted thinking type to the flow of hot lava from a volcano—it only moves about five feet an hour, but it devastates everything in its way.[15]

Inferior extraverted feeling can nevertheless be quite genuine. Being undifferentiated, it is primitive but without calculation—"just as a dog wags its tail," writes von Franz.[16]

Such a person is of course very vulnerable to the love-object. In the film *The Blue Angel,* a middle-aged professor falls in love with a young cabaret dancer, a warm-hearted vamp who turns him into a clown to introduce her act. He loves her so much that he gives up his academic life and is completely ruined. This is a good example of the loyalty of inferior feeling, but also its bad taste.

As mentioned above, the introverted thinker tends to be involved with internal images rather than external facts. In *The Blue Angel,* for instance, the professor is not influenced by the objective reality of the essentially ordinary dancer who fascinates him. She actually does try to warn him off, but with his introverted orientation he cannot get past his own projected image of her; he sees her as the ideal, and nothing she does or says has any effect.

The converse way in which inferior extraverted feeling typically manifests is that others feel devalued and "unseen." Jung notes:

---

15 Ibid., p. 43.
16 Ibid.

What distinguishes [the extraverted thinking type], namely his intense relation to objects, is almost completely lacking in [the introverted thinking type]. . . . If the object is a person, this person has a distinct feeling that he matters only in a negative way; in milder cases he is merely conscious of being *de trop*, but with a more extreme type he feels himself warded off as something definitely disturbing. This negative relation to the object, ranging from indifference to aversion, characterizes every introvert and makes a description of the type exceedingly difficult. Everything about him tends to disappear and get concealed.[17]

Casual acquaintances of introverted thinkers may find them inconsiderate and domineering, but those who appreciate a keen mind tend to value their friendship very highly. In the pursuit of their ideas they are generally stubborn, not amenable to influence. This contrasts strongly with their suggestibility in personal matters; they are typically quite naive and trusting, and so others may easily take advantage of them.

Since they pay scant attention to outer reality, this type is the proverbial "absent-minded professor," the "forgetful Jones." This can be quite charming, but less so the more they become single-mindedly attached to their own ideas or inner images. Then their convictions become rigid and unbending, their judgment cold, inflexible, arbitrary. In the extreme case, they may lose all connection with objective reality and so become isolated from friends, family and colleagues.

This is the difference between extremes of introverted thinking and extraverted thinking. "Whereas the latter sinks to the level of a mere representation of facts," writes Jung, "the former evaporates into a representation of the irrepresentable, far beyond anything that could be expressed in an image."[18]

---

[17] *Psychological Types,* CW 6, par. 633.

[18] Ibid., par. 630.

In both cases, further psychological development is stifled, and the generally positive thinking process usurped by the unconscious effects of the other functions—sensation, intuition and feeling. Normally these are a healthy compensation for one-sided thinking. In the extreme, where their compensatory influence is resisted by consciousness, the whole personality is colored by negativity and primitive affect, bitterness, oversensitivity and misanthropy.

The Introverted Feeling Type

Feeling in the introverted attitude is determined principally by the subjective factor. In its unconcern with the object it is as different from extraverted feeling as is introverted from extraverted thinking.

This type is difficult to understand because so little appears on the surface. According to Jung, the expression "Still waters run deep" applies to such persons.[19] To the extent that they are one-sided, they will seem to have no feeling and no thoughts at all. This is easily misunderstood as coldness or indifference on the one hand, and stupidity on the other.

Jung describes the aim of introverted feeling as "not to adjust itself to the object, but to subordinate it in an unconscious effort to realize the underlying images":

> It is continually seeking an image which has no existence in reality, but which it has seen in a kind of vision. It glides unheedingly over all objects that do not fit in with its aim. It strives after inner intensity, for which the objects serve at most as a stimulus. The depth of this feeling can only be guessed—it can never be clearly grasped. It makes people silent and difficult of access; it shrinks back like a violet from the brute nature of the object in order to fill the depths of the subject. It comes out with negative judgments or as-

---

[19] Ibid., par. 640.

sumes an air of profound indifference as a means of defence.[20]

What is true of introverted thinking is equally true of introverted feeling, only in the former everything is thought, while in the latter it is felt. Both are oriented to inner images rather than outer facts. Images in the introverted thinker are tied to thoughts and ideals; images in the introverted feeling type manifest as values.

Since the introversion of this type inhibits outer expression, such persons are seldom outspoken about what they feel. But their subjective value system, notes von Franz, generally exerts "a positive secret influence on their surroundings":

> Introverted feeling types, for instance, very often form the ethical backbone of a group; without irritating the others by preaching moral or ethical precepts, they themselves have such correct standards of ethical values that they secretly emanate a positive influence on those around them. One has to behave correctly because they have the right kind of value standard, which always suggestively forces one to be decent if they are present. Their differentiated introverted feeling sees what is inwardly the really important factor.[21]

Persons of this type neither shine nor reveal themselves. Their motives, if any, generally remain well hidden. They have an enigmatic air of self-containment. They are inclined to shun parties and large gatherings, not because they judge those who go to them as unimportant or uninteresting (which an extraverted feeling type might assume to be the case), but simply because their evaluative feeling function is numbed when too much comes in at one time. Jung writes:

> They are mostly silent, inaccessible, hard to understand; often they hide behind a childish or banal mask, and their

---

20 Ibid., par. 638.

21 *Jung's Typology*, p. 49.

temperament is inclined to melancholy. . . . Their outward demeanour is harmonious, inconspicuous, giving an impression of pleasing repose, or of sympathetic response, with no desire to affect others, to impress, influence, or change them in any way. . . . Although there is a constant readiness for peaceful and harmonious co-existence . . . there is little effort to respond to the real emotions of the other person. . . . This type observes a benevolent though critical neutrality, coupled with a faint trace of superiority that soon takes the wind out of the sails of a sensitive person.[22]

Extraverts, particularly those whose dominant function is thinking, are completely bemused by the introverted feeling type. The former find the latter at once both peculiar and fascinating. The magnetic attraction is due to the apparent "emptiness"—from the point of view of the extravert—that cries out to be filled. Of course the reverse is also true: the introverted feeling type is naturally drawn to one who mixes easily and is articulate in a group. In each case the other is the personification of the inferior function.[23]

Such encounters are common everyday occurrences, as is the subsequent acrimony. Although with mutual insight there is always the possibility of a lasting relationship, the fascination with one's opposite type, as pointed out in the introduction (see page 30), seldom lasts indefinitely.

Just as introverted thinking is counterbalanced by a kind of primitive feeling, to which objects attach themselves with magical force, introverted feeling is counterbalanced by a primitive, inferior thinking. Since thinking in this type is ex-

---

[22] *Psychological Types,* CW 6, par. 640.

[23] In later life, the attraction is more commonly between the dominant function of one and the auxiliary function of the other. This seems to be a more workable combination, perhaps because the complexes associated with the inferior function are not so easily constellated.

traverted, it tends to be reductive—concretistic, slavishly oriented to facts. This is in fact a normal and healthy compensation that works to mitigate the importance of the subject, for this type is just as inclined to egocentricity as are the other introverted types.

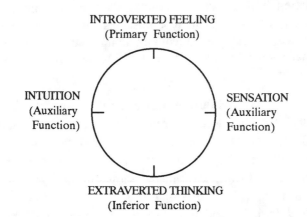

INTROVERTED FEELING
(Primary Function)

INTUITION
(Auxiliary
Function)

SENSATION
(Auxiliary
Function)

EXTRAVERTED THINKING
(Inferior Function)

Unchecked, the ego of the introvert assumes an overriding importance. In this case, writes Jung, "the mysterious power of intensive feeling turns into a banal and overweening desire to dominate, into vanity and despotic bossiness."[24] Where subliminal compensating processes are completely suppressed, the unconscious thinking becomes openly hostile and negative, and gets projected into the environment. Jung describes the result in a woman of this type:

> The egocentrized subject now comes to feel the power and importance of the devalued object. She begins consciously to feel "what other people think." Naturally, other people are thinking all sorts of mean things, scheming evil, contriving plots, secret intrigues, etc. In order to forestall them, she herself is obliged to start counter-intrigues, to

---

24 Ibid., par. 642.

suspect others and sound them out, and weave counter-plots. Beset by rumours, she must make frantic efforts to get her own back and be top dog. . . . even prostitute her virtues in order to play the trump card. Such a state of affairs must end in exhaustion. The form of neurosis is neurasthenic rather than hysterical, often with severe physical complications, such as anaemia and its sequelae.[25]

The Introverted Sensation Type

In the introverted attitude, sensation is based predominantly on the subjective component of perception. Although its very nature makes it dependent on objective stimuli, the sensed object takes second place to the sensing subject.

Sensation is an irrational function, because it is oriented not by a logical process of judgment but simply by what is and what happens. "Whereas the extraverted sensation type is guided by the intensity of objective influences," notes Jung, "the introverted type is guided by the intensity of the subjective sensation excited by the objective stimulus."[26]

The introverted sensation type is like a highly sensitized photographic plate. The physical sensitivity to objects and other people takes in every smallest shade and detail—what they look like, how they feel to the touch, their taste and smell and the sounds they make. Von Franz writes that she first understood this type when Emma Jung gave a paper on intro-verted sensation as her own dominant function.

> When somebody comes into the room, such a type notices the way the person comes in, the hair, the expression on the face, the clothes, and the way the person walks. . . . every detail is absorbed. The impression comes from the

25 Ibid., par. 643.
26 Ibid., par. 650.

object to the subject; it is as though a stone fell into deep water—the impression falls deeper and deeper and sinks in. Outwardly, the introverted sensation type looks utterly stupid. He just sits and stares, and you do not know what is going on within him. He looks like a piece of wood with no reaction at all . . . but inwardly the impression is being absorbed. . . . The quick inner reactions go on underneath, and the outer reaction comes in a delayed way. These are the people who, if told a joke in the morning, will probably laugh at midnight.[27]

Introverted sensation types, if they are creative artists, have a facility for bringing a scene to life in painting or in writing. Thomas Mann, for instance, in describing every detail of a scene, evokes the whole atmosphere of a room or personality. The French Impressionist painters are also in this group; they reproduce exactly the internal impressions stimulated in them by a scene or a person in the real world.

That is the difference between extraverted and introverted sensation. The former, in an artist, would produce a realistic *reflection* of the object, the latter a faithful rendering of the *impression* made by the object on the subject. Jung writes:

Introverted sensation apprehends the background of the physical world rather than its surface. The decisive thing is not the reality of the object, but the reality of the subjective factor, of the primordial images which, in their totality, constitute a psychic mirror-world. It is a mirror with the peculiar faculty of reflecting the existing contents of consciousness not in their known and customary form, but . . . somewhat as a million-year-old consciousness might see them. . . . Introverted sensation transmits an image which does not so much reproduce the object as spread over it the patina of age-old subjective experience . . . . while extra-

---

27 *Jung's Typology,* pp. 27-28.

verted sensation seizes on the momentary existence of things open to the light of day.[28]

The subjective factor in sensation is essentially the same as in the other introverted types. It is an unconscious disposition which alters the sense-perception at its source, thus depriving it of the character of a purely objective influence. Subjective perception is oriented to the meaning that adheres to objects rather than to their inherent physical properties.

The introvert's characteristic difficulty in self-expression is also true of this type. Jung suggests that this conceals the introverted sensation type's essential irrationality:

> On the contrary, he may be conspicuous for his calmness and passivity, or for his rational self-control. This peculiarity, which often leads a superficial judgment astray, is really due to his unrelatedness to objects. Normally the object is not consciously devalued in the least, but its stimulus is removed from it and immediately replaced by a subjective reaction no longer related to the reality of the object. This naturally has the same effect as devaluation. Such a type can easily make one question why one should exist at all, or why objects in general should have any justification for their existence since everything essential still goes on happening without them.[29]

Seen from outside, one often has the impression that the effect of the object does not penetrate into the subject at all. In extreme cases this can be true—the subject is no longer able to distinguish between the real object and the subjective perception—but normally the apparent indifference to the object is simply a means of defense, typical of the introverted attitude, against the intrusion or influence of the outside world.

---

[28] *Psychological Types,* CW 6, par. 649.

[29] Ibid., par. 650.

Without a capacity for artistic expression, impressions sink into the depths and hold consciousness under a spell. Since thinking and feeling are also relatively unconscious, the impressions of the outer world can only be organized in archaic ways. There is little or no rational, judging ability to sort things out. Such a person, according to Jung, "is uncommonly inaccessible to objective understanding, and he usually fares no better in understanding himself."[30]

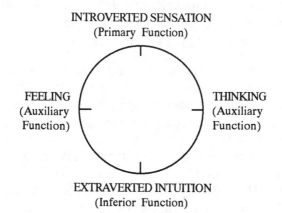

INTROVERTED SENSATION
(Primary Function)

FEELING
(Auxiliary
Function)

THINKING
(Auxiliary
Function)

EXTRAVERTED INTUITION
(Inferior Function)

The inferior extraverted intuition of this type, writes von Franz, "has a very wierd, eerie, fantastic quality . . . concerned with the impersonal, collective outer world."[31] As mentioned earlier, the tendency of sensation is in fact generally to repress intuition, since it interferes with the perception of concrete reality. Hence intuition in this type, when it does manifest, has an archaic character.

> Whereas true extraverted intuition is possessed of singular resourcefulness, a "good nose" for objectively real possibilities, this archaicized intuition has an amazing flair for all the ambiguous, shadowy, sordid, dangerous possibilities

---

[30] Ibid., par. 652.

[31] *Jung's Typology,* p. 81.

lurking in the background. The real and conscious intentions of the object mean nothing to it; instead, it sniffs out every conceivable archaic motive underlying such an intention. It therefore has a dangerous and destructive quality that contrasts glaringly with the well-meaning innocuousness of the conscious attitude.[32]

Unlike extraverted sensation types, who pick up intuitions that concern the subject—themselves—introverted sensation types are more inclined to have dark prophetic fantasies of what might happen in the outside world—to their family or "mankind." They are also prone, notes von Franz, to soul-flooding insights that belie their usual down-to-earth nature:

Such a type might, while walking down a street, see a crystal in a shop window, and his intuition might suddenly grasp its symbolic meaning: the whole symbolic meaning of the crystal would flood into his soul. . . . That would have been triggered off by the outside event, since his inferior intuition is essentially extraverted. Naturally, he has the same bad characteristics of the extraverted sensation type: in both, intuitions are very often of a sinister character, and if not worked upon, therefore, the prophetic contents that break through will be pessimistic and negative.[33]

Although accurate in recording physical reality, the sensation function tends to be sluggish, slow-moving. To the extent that the other functions are unconscious, this type easily gets stuck in a rut, bogged down in the routine of the present moment. Attuned to the here and now, what is, they have the greatest difficulty imagining what might be, the possibilities that are the natural domain of the intuitive.

---

[32] *Psychological Types,* CW 6, par. 654.
[33] *Jung's Typology,* p. 29.

So long as the sensation type does not hold too aloof from the object, writes Jung, "his unconscious intuition has a salutary compensating effect on the rather fantastic and overcredulous attitude of consciousness":

> But as soon as the unconscious becomes antagonistic, the archaic intuitions come to the surface and exert their pernicious influence, forcing themselves on the individual and producing compulsive ideas of the most perverse kind. The result is usually a compulsion neurosis, in which the hysterical features are masked by symptoms of exhaustion.[34]

The Introverted Intuitive Type

Intuition, like sensation, is an irrational function of perception. Where the latter is motivated by physical reality, the former is oriented to psychic reality. In the extraverted attitude, the subjective factor is suppressed, but in the introvert it is decisive. When this way of functioning is dominant, we have an introverted intuitive type.

Introverted intuition is directed to the contents of the unconscious. Although it may be stimulated by external objects, writes Jung, "it does not concern itself with external possibilities but with what the external object has released within."[35] It sees behind the scenes, fastening on, and fascinated by, the inner images that have been brought to life.

Jung gives the example of a man overtaken by an attack of dizziness. Where introverted sensation would note the physical disturbance, perceiving all its qualities, its intensity, its course, how it arose and how long it lasted, introverted intuition would see none of that but rather seek to explore every detail

---

[34] *Psychological Types,* CW 6, par. 654.
[35] Ibid., par. 656.

of the images aroused by the disturbance. "It holds fast to the vision, observing with the liveliest interest how the picture changes, unfolds, and finally fades":

> In this way introverted intuition perceives all the background processes of consciousness with almost the same distinctness as extraverted sensation registers external objects. For intuition, therefore, unconscious images acquire the dignity of things. But, because intuition excludes the co-operation of sensation . . . . the images appear as though detached from the subject, as though existing in themselves without any relation to him. Consequently, in the above-mentioned example, the introverted intuitive, if attacked by vertigo, would never imagine that the image he perceived might in some way refer to himself. To a judging type [thinking or feeling] this naturally seems inconceivable, but it is none the less a fact.[36]

The introverted intuitive type, like the extraverted intuitive, has an uncanny capacity for smelling out the future, the not-yet-manifest possibilities of a situation. But the intuition is directed within, hence they are primarily found among seers and prophets, poets, artists; among primitive peoples they are the shamans who convey the messages of the gods to the tribe.

On a more mundane level, persons of this type tend to be mystical day-dreamers. They do not communicate well, are frequently misunderstood, lack good judgment about both themselves and others, and never accomplish anything. They move from image to image, writes Jung, "chasing after every possibility in the teeming womb of the unconscious," without establishing any personal connection.[37]

This type is especially liable to neglect ordinary physical needs. They often have little awareness of their own bodily

---

[36] Ibid., par. 657.

[37] Ibid., par. 658.

existence or its effect on others. It often appears (especially to the extravert) that reality does not exist for them—they are simply lost in fruitless fantasies. Jung counters this by describing the value of this type to the collective community:

> The perception of the images of the unconscious, produced in such inexhaustible abundance by the creative energy of life, is of course fruitless from the standpoint of immediate utility. But since these images represent possible views of the world which may give life a new potential, this function, which to the outside world is the strangest of all, is as indispensable to the total psychic economy as is the corresponding human type to the psychic life of a people. Had this type not existed, there would have been no prophets in Israel.[38]

Introverted intuitives are characteristically vague about details in the "real" world. They easily get lost in strange cities; they misplace possessions, forget appointments, seldom turn up on time, arrive at airports at the very last minute. Their working environment is usually chaotic; they can't find the right papers, the tools they need, clean clothes. There is seldom anything orderly or tidy about them. They tend to muddle through life, dependent on the tolerance and good will of sensation-oriented friends.

To other types their behavior is often annoying, at best, and at worst burdensome. They themselves may remain unconcerned, pointing out, when pressed, that details "are really not that important."

The aloofness of this type to tangible reality is easily misread as indifference on the one hand and untruthfulness on the other. They are true not to outer facts but to inner images. They may not consciously lie, but their memory or evocation of an event will hardly coincide with so-called objective reali-

---

[38] Ibid.

ty. In the extreme case, a person of this type becomes a complete enigma to friends, and eventually, since they do not feel valued and their opinions don't seem to matter, friends may become thin on the ground.

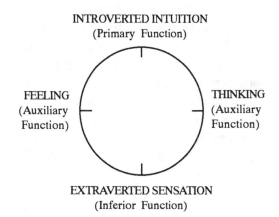

INTROVERTED INTUITION
(Primary Function)

FEELING
(Auxiliary
Function)

THINKING
(Auxiliary
Function)

EXTRAVERTED SENSATION
(Inferior Function)

The extreme introverted intuitive represses both functions of judgment—thinking and feeling—but most of all the sensation of the object. This naturally gives rise to compensatory extraverted sensation of an archaic nature. The unconscious personality, writes Jung, "can best be described as an extraverted sensation type of a rather low and primitive order":

Instinctuality and intemperance are the hallmarks of this sensation, combined with an extraordinary dependence on sense-impressions. This compensates the rarefied air of the intuitive's conscious attitude, giving it a certain weight, so that complete "sublimation" is prevented. But if, through a forced exaggeration of the conscious attitude, there should be a complete subordination to inner perceptions, the unconscious goes over to the opposition, giving rise to compulsive sensations whose excessive dependence on the object directly contradicts the conscious attitude. The form of neurosis is a compulsion neurosis with hypochondriacal symptoms, hypersensitivity of the sense organs, and compulsive ties to particular persons or objects.[39]

According to von Franz, the introverted intuitive has particular trouble in the area of sex.[40] Such types are not the world's greatest lovers, simply because they have so little sense of what is happening in their own bodies or that of their partners. At the same time, they are inclined to have a prurient nature—reflecting the inferior and therefore primitive sensation function—and through lack of judgment will come out with coarse and socially inappropriate sexual allusions.

Jung acknowledges that although both the introverted intuitive and the introverted sensation type are, from an extraverted and rationalistic standpoint, "indeed the most useless of men," the way they function is nevertheless instructive:

> Viewed from a higher standpoint, they are living evidence that this rich and varied world with its overflowing and intoxicating life is not purely external, but also exists within. . . . In their own way, they are educators and promoters of culture. Their life teaches more than their words. From their lives, and not least from their greatest fault—their inability to communicate—we may understand one of the greatest errors of our civilization, that is, the superstitious belief in verbal statements, the boundless overestimation of instruction by means of words and methods.[41]

---

[39] Ibid., par. 663.
[40] *Jung's Typology*, p. 35.
[41] *Psychological Types*, CW 6, par. 665.

4

Concluding Remarks

Why Typology?

No system of typology is ever more than a gross indicator of what people have in common and the differences between them. Jung's model is no exception. It is distinguished solely by its parameters—the two attitudes and the four functions. What it does not and cannot show, nor does it pretend to, is the uniqueness of the individual.

No one is a pure type. It would be foolish to even try to reduce an individual personality to this or that, just one thing or another. In terms of Jung's model, each of us is a conglomeration, an admixture of the attitudes and functions that in their combination defy classification. All that is true, and emphatically acknowledged by Jung—

> One can never give a description of a type, no matter how complete, that would apply to more than one individual, despite the fact that in some ways it aptly characterizes thousands of others. Conformity is one side of a man, uniqueness is the other.[1]

—but it does not obviate the practical value of his model, particularly in clinical situations where a person has run aground on the shoals of his or her own psychology. Without a model of some kind, we are simply adrift in a morass of individual opinions—lost in a jungle without a compass.

> It is not the purpose of a psychological typology to classify human beings into categories—this in itself would be pretty

---

[1] *Psychological Types,* CW 6, par. 895.

pointless. Its purpose is rather to provide a critical psychology which would make a methodical investigation and presentation of the empirical material possible. First and foremost, it is a critical tool for the research worker, who needs definite points of view and guidelines if he is to reduce the chaotic profusion of individual experiences to any kind of order. . . . Secondly, a typology is a great help in understanding the wide variations that occur among individuals, and it also furnishes a clue to the fundamental differences in the psychological theories now current. Last but not least, it is an essential means for determining the "personal equation" of the practising psychologist, who, armed with an exact knowledge of his differentiated and inferior functions, can avoid many serious blunders in dealing with his patients.[2]

Whether Jung's model is "true" or not—objectively true—is a moot point (is anything ever "objectively" true?). Certainly, the extent to which the two attitudes and the four functions accord with statistical reality has not been established. To do that, one would have to correlate tests of millions of people with great insight into themselves, and even then the results would be suspect, since the testing procedure itself would still depend on the typology of those who formulated the test—the questions, phrasing, preconceptions, assumptions, etc.—not to mention the circumstantial vagaries that attend any test at a specific time.

The real "truth" is that Jung's model of psychological types has all the advantages and disadvantages of any scientific model. Although lacking statistical verification, it is equally hard to disprove. But it accords with experiential reality. Moreover, since it is based on a fourfold—mandala-like—way of looking at things that is archetypal, it is *psychologically satisfying.*

---

[2] Ibid., par. 986.

As mentioned earlier (page 31), a person's behavior can be quite misleading in determining typology. For instance, to enjoy being with other people is characteristic of the extraverted attitude, but this does not automatically mean that a person who enjoys lots of company is an extraverted type.

Naturally, a person's activities will to some extent be determined by typology, but the interpretation of those activities in terms of typology depends on the value system behind the action. Where the subject—oneself—and a personal value system are the dominant motivating factors, there is by definition an introverted type, whether at a party or alone. Similarly, when one is predominantly oriented to the object—things and other people—there is an extraverted type, whether in a crowd or on one's own. This is what makes Jung's system primarily a model of *personality* rather than behavior.

Everything psychic is relative. I cannot say, think or do anything that is not colored by my particular way of seeing the world, which in turn is a manifestation of my typology. This psychological "rule" is analogous to Einstein's famous theory of relativity in physics, and equally as significant.

Being consciously aware of the way I tend to function makes it possible for me to assess my attitudes and behavior in a given situation and adjust them accordingly. It enables me both to compensate for my personal disposition and to be tolerant of someone who does not function as I do—someone who has, perhaps, a strength or facility I myself lack.

From this point of view, the important question is not whether one is introverted or extraverted, or which function is superior or inferior, but, more pragmatically: in *this* situation, or with *that* person, how did I function? With what effect? Did my actions and the way I expressed myself truly reflect my judgments (thinking and feeling) and perceptions (sensation and intuition)? And if not, why not? What complexes were activated in me? To what end? How and why did I mess things up? What does this say about my psychology? What can I do about it? What do I *want* to do about it?

Type Testing

Although Jung did not foresee the current commercial use of his model of typology,[3] he did warn against its misuse as "a practical guide to a good judgment of human character":

> Even in medical circles the opinion has got about that my method of treatment consists in fitting patients into this system and giving them corresponding "advice." . . . My typology is far rather a critical apparatus serving to sort out and organize the welter of empirical material, but not in any sense to stick labels on people . . . . It is not a physiognomy and not an anthropological system, but a critical psychology dealing with the organization and delimiting of psychic processes that can be shown to be typical.[4]

Typological analysis determined by written tests can be helpful, but it can also be misleading. Such tests are collectively based and static; that is, their validity is statistical and time-specific. They may give a reasonable picture of one's conscious predilections at the time of the test, but in ignoring the dynamic nature of the psyche they say nothing about the possibility of change.

In the corporate world, type tests can be a useful tool to illustrate both the psychological basis of conflicts between individuals in a group and the complementary nature of different personalities. They may also show quite accurately, as

---

[3] The most widely used type tests based on Jungian principles are the Myers-Briggs Type Indicator, the Gray-Wheelwright Type Survey and the Singer-Loomis Inventory. According to *Fortune* magazine ("Personality Tests Are Back," March 30, 1987, pp. 74ff), "some 1.5 million people" took the Myers-Briggs test in 1986.

[4] *Psychological Types,* CW 6, pp. xiv-xv.

measured on the day of the test, the possibility that a particular person will or will not fit, at that time, the requirements of a particular job or environment. But for how long? To whose benefit? And how detrimentally to the individual's other possibilities? Or to the future needs of the corporation?

Type tests do not show the extent to which one's type may have been falsified or perverted by familial and environmental factors; they say nothing about the way in which one's usual way of functioning may be determined by complexes; and they do not reflect the ever-present compensating attitude of the unconscious. In addition, the person taking the test may be using one of the secondary or auxiliary functions to answer the questions—or indeed, responding out of the shadow or persona (see next section).

Above all, type tests do not take into account the experiential reality that a person's typological preferences can change over time.

Take, for instance, a man who has acquired several academic degrees, even a doctorate. Such a person, habituated to long periods of solitary work using the thinking function, might very well show up on a written test as an introverted thinking type. He may even believe himself to be one. But is he really?

Not necessarily. He may have labored for years to fulfil the expectations of others; he may have repressed his longing for extraverted activity to the point where he himself hardly knows it exists. Extraversion and, say, the feeling function, may be buried so deeply in his shadow that only a major life crisis, precipitating a nervous breakdown, would uncover it.

Similarly, a woman who is apparently a feeling type, a homemaker with an active social life, may one day discover the introverted world of ideas and go on to take a university degree. Was she a so-called false type, never given the opportunity to develop her naturally dominant thinking function?

Or is thinking now simply a temporary aberration? Would results of a type test be relevant at either point in her life?

The bottom line is that an externally evaluated test, even though self-administered, is not a reliable guide to what is going on inside. In the area of typology, as with any attempt to understand oneself, there is no substitute for prolonged self-reflection.

Although this is self-evident to the introvert, who is used to, and depends on, reflection, it is rarely so clear to the extravert, who is predisposed to trust, and rely on, determinants in the external world.

Typology and the Shadow

Jung's model of typology is based on preferential or habitual ways of functioning. Used responsibly, it is a valuable guide to our dominant psychological disposition, the way we mostly are. It also reveals, by inference, the way we mostly *aren't* — but could also be.

Where, then, is the rest of us (mostly)?

Theoretically, we can say that the inferior or undeveloped attitude and functions are part of that side of ourselves Jung called the shadow. The reason for this is both conceptual and pragmatic.

Conceptually, the shadow, like the ego, is a complex. But where the ego, as the dominant complex of consciousness, is associated with aspects of oneself that are more or less known (as "I"), the shadow is comprised of personality characteristics that are not part of one's usual way of being in the world, and therefore more or less alien to one's sense of personal identity.[5]

The shadow is potentially both creative and destructive: creative in that it represents aspects of oneself that have been

---

[5] See Jung, "The Shadow," *Aion,* CW 9ii, pars. 13ff.

buried or that might yet be realized; destructive in the sense that its value system and motivations tend to undermine or disturb one's conscious image of oneself.

Everything that is not ego is relatively unconscious; before the contents of the unconscious have been differentiated, the shadow *is* the unconscious. Since the opposite attitude and the inferior functions are by definition relatively unconscious, they are naturally tied up with the shadow.

In one's immediate world, there are attitudes and behavior that are socially acceptable, and those that are not. In our formative years it is natural to repress, or suppress, the unacceptable aspects of ourselves. They "fall into" the shadow. What is left is the persona—the "I" one presents to the outside world.

The persona would live up to what is expected, what is proper. It is both a useful bridge socially and an indispensable protective covering; without a persona, we are simply too vulnerable to others. We regularly cover up our inferiorities with a persona, since we do not like our weaknesses to be seen. (The introverted thinking type at a noisy party may grit his teeth but smile. The extraverted feeling type may pretend to be studying when she's really climbing the wall for lack of company.)

Civilized society, life as we know it, depends on interactions between people through the persona. But it is psychologically unhealthy to identify with it, to believe we are "nothing but" the person we show to others.

Generally speaking, the shadow is less civilized, more primitive, cares little for social propriety. What is of value to the persona is anathema to the shadow, and vice versa. Hence the shadow and the persona function in a compensatory way: the brighter the light, the darker the shadow. The more one identifies with the persona—which in effect is to deny that one has a shadow—the more trouble one will have with the unacknowledged "other side" of the personality.

Thus the shadow constantly challenges the morality of the persona, and, to the extent that ego-consciousness identifies with the persona, the shadow also threatens the ego. In the process of psychological development that Jung called individuation, disidentification from the persona and the conscious assimilation of the shadow go hand in hand. The ideal is to have an ego strong enough to acknowledge both persona and shadow without identifying with either of them.

This is not as easy as it sounds. We tend to identify with what we are good at, and why shouldn't we? The superior function, after all, has an undeniable utilitarian value. It greases the wheels, life runs smoothly; it generally brings praise, material rewards, a degree of satisfaction. It inevitably becomes a prominent aspect of the persona. Why give it up? The answer is that we don't—unless we have to. And when do we "have to"?—when we encounter situations in life that are not amenable to the way we usually function; that is, when the way we tend to look at things doesn't work.

In practice, as noted earlier, the shadow and everything associated with it is virtually synonomous with *unlived life.* "There is more to life than this," is a remark heard often in the analyst's office. All that I consciously am and aspire to be effectively shuts out what I might be, could be, *also am.* Some of what I "also am" has been or is repressed because it was—or is—environmentally unacceptable; some is simply unrealized potential.

Through introspection, we can become aware of shadow aspects of the personality, but we may still resist them or fear their influence. And even where they are known and would be welcome, they are not readily available to the conscious will. For instance, I may be well aware that my intuition is shadowy —primitive and unadapted—but not be able to call it up when it's needed. I may know that feeling is required in a particular situation but for the life of me can't muster it. I want to enjoy the party but my carefree extraverted side has vanished. I may know I'm due for some solitary introversion, but the lure of the bright lights is just too much.

The shadow does not necessarily demand equal time with the ego, but for a balanced personality it does require recognition. For the introvert this may involve an occasional night on the town—against one's "better judgment." For the extravert it might involve—in spite of oneself—an evening staring at the wall. In general, the person whose shadow is dormant gives the impression of being stodgy, lifeless. Typologically, this works both ways: the extravert seems to lack depth; the introvert appears socially inept.

The introvert's psychological situation is laid bare in Franz Kafka's observation:

> Whoever leads a solitary life, and yet now and then wants to attach himself somewhere; whoever, according to changes in the time of day, the weather, the state of his business and the like, suddenly wishes to see any arm at all to which he might cling—he will not be able to manage for long without a window looking on to the street.[6]

Similarly, the extravert may only become conscious of the shadow when struck by the vacuity of social intercourse.

There is a balance between introversion and extraversion, as there is between the normally opposing functions, but it rarely becomes necessary—or even possible—to seek it out, until and unless the conscious ego-personality falls on its face.

In that case, which happily manifests as a nervous breakdown rather than a more serious psychotic break, the shadow side demands to be recognized. The resulting turmoil may not feel so good, and may upset many things one has known or believed about oneself, but it has the advantage of overcoming the tyranny of the dominant attitude of consciousness. If the

---

[6] "The Street Window," in *The Penal Colony,* trans. Willa and Edwin Muir (New York: Schocken Books, 1961), p. 39.

symptoms are then attended to with some seriousness, the whole personality can be enlivened.

There is by definition a natural conflict between ego and shadow, but when one has made a commitment to live out as much of one's potential as possible, then the integration of the shadow—including the inferior attitude and functions—from being merely theoretically desirable, becomes a practical necessity. Hence the process of assimilating the shadow requires the capacity to live with some psychological tension.

The introverted man, for instance, under the influence of his inferior extraverted shadow, is prone to imagine he is missing something: vivacious women, fast company, excitement. He himself may see these as chimeras, but his shadow yearns for them. His shadow will lead him into the darkest venues, and then, as often as not (whimsically), abandon him. What is left? A lonely introvert who longs for home.

On the other hand, the extraverting introvert who is taken at face value—as a true extravert—is liable to end up in hot water. Whereas the introverting extravert has only himself to deal with, the extraverting introvert often makes a tremendous impact on those who cross his path, but he might not want to be with them the next day. When his introversion reasserts itself, he may literally want nothing to do with other people. Thus the introverted intellectual whose shadow is a carefree Don Juan wreaks havoc on the hearts of unsuspecting women.

True extraverts genuinely enjoy being part of the crowd. That is their natural home. They are restless alone, not because they are avoiding themselves, but because they have no parameters for establishing their identity outside of the group. The introverted shadow of extraverts encourages them to stay home and find out who they are. But just as introverts may be abandoned by their shadows in a noisy bar, so extraverts may be left high and dry—and lonely—when on their own.

The opposite attitude and the inferior functions regularly appear as shadow figures in dreams and fantasies. According to Jung's understanding, all the characters that appear in dreams are personifications of aspects of the dreamer.[7] Dream activity becomes heightened when a function not usually available to consciousness is required. Thus a man who is a thinking type, after a quarrel with his wife, for instance, may be assailed in his dreams by images of primitive feeling persons, dramatically illustrating a side of himself he needs to acknowledge. Similarly, the sensation type stuck in a rut may be confronted in dreams by an intuitive type showing some possible ways out, and so on.

To assimilate a function, a subject broached above in the introduction (page 22), means to live with it in the foreground of consciousness. "If one does a little cooking or sewing," writes von Franz, "it does not mean that the sensation function has been assimilated":

> Assimilation means that the whole conscious adaptation of conscious life, for a while, lies on that one function. Switching over to an auxiliary function takes place when one feels that the present way of living has become lifeless, when one gets more or less constantly bored with oneself and one's activities. . . . The best way to know how to switch is simply to say, "All right, all this is now completely boring, it does not mean anything to me any more. Where in my past life is an activity that I feel I could still enjoy? An activity out of which I could still get a kick?" If a person then genuinely picks up that activity, he will see that he has switched over to another function.[8]

—and, to some extent, assimilated an aspect of the shadow.

*

---

[7] See "General Aspects of Dream Psychology," and "On the Nature of Dreams," *The Structure and Dynamics of the Psyche,* CW 8.

[8] *Lectures on Jung's Typology* (Zurich: Spring Publications, 1971), p. 60.

The final word here must be that aside from the clinical implications of Jung's model of typology, its major importance continues to be the perspective it offers the individual on his or her own personality.

Using Jung's model in a personally meaningful way requires the same kind of dedicated reflection as does getting a handle on one's shadow and any of the other complexes. In other words, it involves paying close attention, over an extended period of time, to where one's energy tends to go, the motivations that lie behind one's behavior, and the problems that arise in relationships with others.

Modern technology has provided us with many useful tools, quick and easy ways to accomplish what would otherwise be onerous or time-consuming tasks. The process of understanding oneself, however, is not amenable to short cuts. It remains intractably linked to, and enriched by, individual effort.

Appendix 1

The Clinical Significance of Extraversion and Introversion

H.K. Fierz, M.D.[1]

Extraversion and introversion are typical, constitutional attitudes. The primary interest of the extravert lies in the object, that of the introvert in the subject.

If we wish to study the possible medical consequences of these two basic attitudes, we must first understand the moment at which subject and object arise.

Subject and object always appear when relationships which have hitherto been governed by a *participation mystique* are exposed to criticism, whether from the subject himself or from someone else.[2] Such an event may affect the whole personality, for instance, in the young child, or in largely uncon-

---

[1] H.K. Fierz was medical director of the Zurich Clinic and Research Center for Jungian Psychology *(Klinik am Zurichberg)* for more than twenty years, until his death in 1985. He was also a training analyst at the C.G. Jung Institute in Zurich.

This article was originally published in German in *Acte psychotherapeutica,* 1959. The English translation first appeared in *Current Trends in Analytical Psychology* (Proceedings of the 1st International Congress for Analytical Psychology, 1958), ed. Gerhard Adler (London: Tavistock Press, 1961).

[2] [The term *participation mystique,* derived from the anthropologist Lucien Lévy-Bruhl and used frequently by Jung, denotes a primitive unconscious connection in which one cannot clearly distinguish oneself from other people. This is what lies behind the natural phenomenon of projection, in which one sees in someone else characteristics that are actually one's own. See Jung, "Definitions," *Psychological Types,* CW 6, par. 781.—D.S.]

scious, undifferentiated people. But even in differentiated adults we still find unconscious areas in need of development. This situation is conducive to conflicts that may provoke criticism and thus lead to the dissolution of a *participation mystique*.

By conflict we understand that two persons in a given relationship find that they are not in complete harmony. The individual who experiences this disturbance of harmony is the subject and the partner to the conflict, with whom he feels in disharmony, is his object.

We can observe how this disturbance manifests itself in the individual: an affect is created, involving an animus-anima problem. There is also a disturbance of adjustment to the now objectivated environment, which creates further effects, constellating the problem of the shadow.

A classic example can be found in young children: they discover that the parents are not always as perfect as they had expected. The affect created is anger with the parents: the ensuing churlishness leads to a problem of adjustment. The child is now exposed to doubts such as: "Who am I?", or "Who are my parents?" And further, "What is this I?", "What is 'father', 'mother'?" In this way subject and object are born. This situation soon constellates the parental archetypes, hence the often considerable energy of the affect.

The same problem arises for everyone when a *participation mystique* is dissolved. Although the problem is a general one, the way it is worked through varies according to whether the primary interest is directed towards the subject or object. The individual way in which the problem is solved indicates the basic attitude.

The introvert is primarily concerned with the subject, and so he becomes aware of the disturbing factors in the subject. At this point the affect arises. He has a tendency to damp down this affect, and devotes himself to this task with alacrity by seeking a new and reassuring orientation. His difficulty in external adjustment to the object is less—or not at all—important to him. For this reason the introvert frequently appears as negative, "shadowy", showing himself as odd, whimsical, haughty, or even malicious.

This difficulty will not be dealt with by greater awareness, and realization, but by evasion. An introvert may thus systematically reduce his circle of acquaintances by selection of the most "harmless". But he often comes up against the reality of the external world. The "malice of the object" can be his stumbling-block: he will always have "bad luck". Even a young introvert may break his leg on the stairs. He could not pay attention to the stairs, but had to express his anger at the horrible red colour of the stair carpet (with the object of being able to say later "I don't mind what the colour is" or perhaps "I don't like this red because it doesn't suit me").

Naturally it does him good to let out his affect. The emotion subsides and he is thus, for instance, protected against metabolic disturbance. It is more likely that the surgeon will be called in, although mainly for minor or only moderately serious interventions.

At this stage of development it would seem that the spirit is satisfied but the instinct neglected. Mentally "superior", but alienated from his surroundings, the introvert comes into perpetual collision with the world, though usually without endangering his life. It is perhaps possible that the introvert—in order to remain calm and aloof from the world—breathes in an inadequate and inhibited way, and thus may become relatively easily susceptible to pulmonary tuberculosis.

The extravert is primarily concerned with the object. He likes to organize his object relationships. He gives himself up to them, and has anything but a "shadowy" appearance. He overlooks the fact that something is happening inside him, that something has been set in motion. In spite of the extravert's successful adaptation to the object, this oversight becomes apparent from time to time when the underestimated affect manifests itself in occasional changes of mood that soon develop into animosity.

The unrealized affect can also influence the metabolism: liver troubles are typical and even the heart may be affected. At this stage of development he is more likely to need the physician than the surgeon. Generally speaking there is no danger to life when the extravert follows his instinct and neglects the spiritual side.

This first stage of development is, however, followed by another. In the case of the introvert, the lack of external adaptation increases. In spite of all attempts at "escaping inwards", and in spite of his endeavour to restrict the number of objects by selection, he may come into such a collision with the world that the reality of the object is forced upon him. And now the affect can no longer be pacified: it manifests itself clearly, and the introvert shows his animosity usually much more bitterly than the harmless extravert.

The extravert, on the other hand, reaches a point where his affect clamours for satisfaction. The affect breaks through with violence, the adjustment to the external world is shattered and a dark shadow side becomes evident. The extravert is faced with the question of the subject, of the reality of his own person.

In such a situation the introvert should become more extraverted and direct his interests towards the object. And the extravert should become more introverted and turn towards his own humble person, the subject. When the task of reversal of attitudes is not accepted, clinical developments will follow.

For there follows a stubborn and one-sided attempt to cling to the original attitude type. But this is now outmoded, has lost energy to the opposite attitude, and the struggle ends with an *abaissement du niveau mental*.[3] The originally

---

[3] [*Abaissement du niveau mental,* a phenomenon described by the French physician Pierre Janet and adopted by Jung, indicates a lowering of the

superior attitude no longer functions reliably and has become inferior. The break up of the old system has its physical consequences.

The introvert becomes liable to sudden and dangerous infections. The excessive affect can disturb his metabolism so seriously that a highly dangerous, even pernicious, condition may arise. The danger comes from within: the introvert needs the physician, for his life may be in danger.

For the extravert also there is grave danger if he tries to maintain his one-sided, outmoded, primary attitude. His adaptation to external reality is no longer reliable. Now he can have accidents and be in need of the surgeon. The surgical intervention needed will be serious, for the accidents that occur to a "decompensating extravert" are usually severe (car or mountaineering accidents).

However it is not always the surgeon who has to help, as the problem often impinges on the legal sphere. Blindness to the subjective side and to the black shadow often lead him into bankruptcy, swindling, and other delinquencies. Thus the extravert may endanger his life through an accident or stupid misdemeanour. . . it does not need capital punishment to destroy a life: prison or Borstal[4] may do it equally well.

This stage of development is critical. The introvert can evade the crisis by suicide. This occurs under pressure of a sudden affect, panic at the power of the hated affect which ruins his subjective tranquility. The extravert may also evade the problem by suicide. He plans his suicide with the delibera-

---

level of consciousness, such as occurs in depression, in sleep and through the use of alcohol or other drugs. In the current context it refers to a psychological situation in which the dominant attitude of consciousness has been defrocked, so to speak. See above, page 24.—D.S.]

[4] [Borstal is the name used in England for "correctional institute" or "reform school," a low-security place of confinement for juveniles in trouble with the law.—D.S.]

tion of the dark shadow, and can thus avoid having to deal with the loss of the beloved object—security.

In this crisis the introvert develops all the symptoms of the extravert, but to a much more menacing degree. Precisely because he will not accept his extraverted side, it appears as automatism, in archaic form, and with more intractable problems. However, these dangerous disorders can nowadays be handled much more successfully than 20 years ago. Dangerous infections respond to treatment by antibiotics. Disturbances formerly fatal to the metabolism yield to drugs such as Serpasil and Largactil.

There is, however, a danger of mental death when the excessive affect disturbs the metabolism to such an extent that mental deterioration occurs; there is also a danger of physical death when the force of the affect destroys the resistance to infection. Again, the danger comes from within.

The extravert, in his crisis, develops in exaggerated form the symptoms of the introvert, as his not realized introversion takes over in dangerously archaic form. If the extravert has come into collision with the world through an accident and been badly injured, the technical improvements in modern surgery, particularly in the highly developed technique of anaesthetics, can help a good deal: rehabilitation by orthopaedic surgery can restore to active life many who would otherwise have been permanently crippled.

When the shadow has brought the extravert into conflict with the world with legal consequences, we must bear in mind that capital punishment is falling increasingly into disuse, and that it is becoming more customary to use a penal sentence for education and not for destructive purposes. Yet there is still danger to life coming, whether from accident or punishment, from without. The accident may kill, or social annihilation may destroy, spiritual life.

There are also formal manifestations of the inferiority of the introvert's extraversion, for instance, in perception. He may intuit, fascinated by the outer world, but the intuition is of poor quality. Thus he does not perceive possibilities as they present themselves to a differentiated intuition, but only "impossible possibilities". From this to paranoia is only a short step. If perception takes place through sensation, the outer world is not understood in an organized manner, but in a disordered way. Here too the condition is often pathological.

The inferior introversion of the extravert manifests itself in the fact that although he is compelled to consideration of, and reflection on, the subject, this often turns into a helpless state of anxiety, largely owing to the lack of discrimination. In reflecting upon himself he takes *pars pro toto*,[5] and rejects himself completely for a single shortcoming. A sense of guilt and sin amounting to mania may then arise. Further, although perfectly aware of the autonomy of personal development, he looks upon it as a catastrophe. The overall picture is one of depression. Sometimes the fascination of the subject gives way again to the original extraversion, which now, however, has become inferior and manifests itself as mania.

It therefore becomes clear that the inferior attitude in the introvert tends to the development of schizophrenic states, whereas in the extravert they may induce manic-depressive ones.

If psychotic symptoms are manifest, then the constellation of the inferior attitude becomes particularly impressive. One need only listen to what they say. When an introvert directs his attention outwards, he may show paranoid reactions. His morbid fascination by the object shows itself in such ruminations as: "He did it, he may, he must not, he should, he will." In this way the inferiority of the extraversion is projected on to

---

[5] [= the part for the whole. Here it refers to what Jung called negative inflation, where one identifies with one's worst characteristics. See *Aion,* CW 9ii, par. 114, and "The Psychology of the Child Archetype," *The Archetypes and the Collective Unconscious,* CW 9i, par. 304.—D.S.]

the object: the other side is therefore bad, stupid, or contemptible. On the other hand, if the extravert, who ought to introvert, becomes depressed, we find his thoughts revolving interminably around the subject. He says: "I did it, I should, I am." And the inferiority of the introversion is thrust on to the subject. So the depressive patient considers himself guilty, unworthy, miserable and impoverished.

Psychiatric experience also sheds a useful light on the two types. It is well known that in schizophrenic cases the psychiatrist orders the earliest possible discharge from the clinic, the so-called "early release", whereas with manic-depressive cases a retardation of the discharge is indicated. Relating this to the problem of the inferior attitude, we could say: the schizophrenic, who is primarily introverted and is displaying an inferior extraversion in his illness, should be sent out into the world to exercise his extraversion. But the manic-depressive, of extraverted disposition, should stay long enough in the clinic to have an opportunity of practising his still undeveloped introversion.

However clearly the psychopathological case may demonstrate certain problems, it is, of course, abnormal. In normal cases the problem of the inferior attitude becomes constellated with the second half of life. But in pathological cases it often presents itself very much earlier. One of the reasons for this may be that family or environmental influences may have led to an early distortion of the original character.

It may be that a constitutional extravert has had an introverted attitude that is quite alien to him forced on him, and the opposite tendency of development aims at restoring the genuine attitude as soon as possible. This clash between a healthy, yet undeveloped extraversion and a distorted, basically alien introverted consciousness, can lead to a very complex, even pathological state. An introvert can be subjected to a corresponding distortion. The details of this problem have not yet been sufficiently studied. I believe, however, that the distortion of the constitutional attitude by environmental factors is one of the principal sources of psychotic symptoms and of the so-called psychopathic pattern.

It would, of course, be ideal if the normal development of the opposite tendency were to take place without disturbance. But, in medicine and particularly in psychology, we seldom observe such cases, as a normal development leaves little to be observed. Where there are disturbances, naturally every shade and variety is forthcoming.

One might add a few further details: the introvert, who has to develop his extraversion, is relatively liable to peptic ulcers. In extraverts, who should introvert, there is, in my experience, a danger of premature arterio-sclerosis. It is well known that sufferers from peptic ulcer may derive relief of symptoms from psychotherapy. But it is perhaps less well known that even relatively serious arterio-sclerotic conditions can be helped considerably by suitable psychotherapy, despite the defeatist psychiatric prognoses to be found in all text books. So that in the case of an extravert who has to work out his introversion, and has become depressive, arterio-sclerotic symptoms should not be allowed to influence the prognosis too seriously, and psychotherapy should by no means be neglected.

Let me sum up the effect of the two basic attitude types from the medical aspect:

The introvert lives primarily in his affect and comes into conflict with the world. He is liable to slight or moderately serious accidents. The extravert adapts himself to the world and neglects the affect. For him the danger lies in the heart and metabolic system. Both attitude types are then, sooner or later, faced with the same problem, to develop the opposite, inferior attitude within themselves.

If this development is inadequate, serious, even fatal disorders may ensue. The introvert may be affected by infections or by pernicious disturbances of the metabolism. The extravert is liable to dangerous accidents and to conflicts with the law. Further, the introvert is liable to peptic ulcers and the extravert to arterio-sclerosis. The introvert's fascinated absorption in the outer world may lead to paranoid symptoms, that of the extravert with the inner world may lead to a manifestation of his inferior introversion in melancholia.

With regard to the psychiatric aspects, we should also stress that the spontaneous, original, primary relationship remains apparent even in crisis (as well as in the constitutional types so ably described by Kretschmer). When the asthenic schizophrenic turns outwards in a hallucinatory way, his spontaneous inclination is towards the subject, and his affective rapport with the external world is correspondingly poor. And when the pyknic melancholic directs his attention inwards, he still remains spontaneously directed towards the object, and his affective rapport is good.[6]

It is impressive to note how—in spite of the resistance set up by the established consciousness—the psychosis helps the inferior attitude to break through. The introverted schizophrenic is brought into contact with the outer world through outbursts of aggression. And the extraverted melancholic shuts himself away from the world in order to develop the idea that no one can understand him, no one wants to understand him, and no one can help him: so he is thrust back upon himself.

We should now ask what treatment is to be expected from a modern medical understanding of the problems of the two attitude types. Generally speaking, it goes without saying that internal, surgical and psychiatric complications appearing in the course of development are to be treated according to the general rules of medical science and experience. But, in addition, it is important in diagnosis to think of the patient as a

---

[6] [Pyknic denotes a short, stocky stature (endomorphic); asthenic refers to a slender, lightly muscled physique.—D.S.]

human being who has to achieve, through his crisis, an acceptance of his inferior other side.

This critical situation creates special dangers requiring particular care and close attention. If, for instance, the inner stability of the introvert breaks down, his whole system may be invaded by infection with unexpected suddenness. Antibiotics must be administered in good time, or it may be too late. In doubtful cases there must therefore be a regular count of leucocytes—records of pulse and temperature are not enough. If the count exceeds 10,000, antibiotic therapy must begin at once. If, on the other hand, the external adaptation of the extravert breaks down, the increased risk of accidents must be guarded against. Mountaineering, for instance, should be forbidden and perhaps even driving a car.

But apart from such special medical care, an understanding of the psychological meaning of the symptomatology is also required, whether the syptoms be physical or psychological. Illness is symptomatic of something aberrant and inferior. In this aberration and inferiority we must recognize the struggle of a human being trying to work out the problems of his opposite attitude. So, in this sense, the medical syptoms are to be interpreted positively, that is, not as morbid aberrations but as a path to wholeness.

Appendix 2

A Dinner Party with the Types

[The following scenario, freely adapted from the original, illustrates in a light vein how Jung's model of typology might look in everyday life.][1]

The Extraverted Feeling Type

Our hostess is a feeling type. Who else would go to the trouble of bringing this group together? Even the invitations—elegantly handwritten on beautiful stationery—express her joy at gathering together these dear friends.

She is a charming woman, warm and voluptuous as a Renoir painting, a marvelous housekeeper, open minded, obliging, worldly. She is very attractive and hospitable, offering fine food beautifully prepared and presented. Her home shows great taste.

Since she tends to repeat the opinions of her husband and father, her conversation is not particularly exciting. Sometimes her views are those of religious leaders or other well-known personalities in her community. In all cases she expresses them with the greatest conviction, as if they originated with her. She does not realize that her only real contribution to the evening—other than the food—is the emotional tone associated with what she says.

---

[1] [First published in German as *Das Diner der Psychologischen Typen* (The Dinner Party of the Psychological Types), in Sammlung Dalp, *Handschriften-deutung* (The Interpretation of Handwriting) (Bern: Franke Verlage, 1952). I am grateful to Magdalena Zillinger for her translation and to Vicki Cowan for the adaptation.—D.S.]

She married a connoisseur—an aesthete—who puts great value on living a life of unobtrusive luxury.

The Introverted Sensation Type

Our host is an art historian and collector. But thinking is for him an inferior function, so although he collects books and owns an impressive collection, he does not delve deeply into their content.

He is tall, dark and lean, as silent as his wife is talkative. He seems to barricade himself behind his wife's chatter. He cannot fathom her dedication to these dinner parties which force him to abandon his beautiful, quiet study. However, they have agreed that she will organize the social side of their life and he knows from long experience that she is a master at the art of entertaining. She is the one who brings needed extraversion to their marriage and connects them to the outside world.

He greets his guests in an elegant way, a bit restrained, and offers his slender hand to the well-known lawyer just coming in. In actual fact, he despises this woman, who is an extraverted thinking type. In greeting her, he mistakenly says, "Goodbye." The hostess, who observes this gaffe with horror, tries to make up for it with a double dose of friendliness.

The Extraverted Thinking Type

The lawyer is the first guest to arrive. Being very concerned with her social position, she would never forgive herself if she were late.

Having recently graduated with honors, she is at the beginning of a promising career as a defense lawyer. Already she has achieved some status as a speaker. Her judgment is accurate and her logic indisputable. Her arguments are based on accepted, concrete facts, speculative ideas being alien to her. As with most extraverted thinking types, she is conservative and places great importance on objective data. Since her auxiliary function is sensation, she is also practical and well organized in both her personal and professional life.

Of her true feelings we know very little. It is said that eventually she will marry the boss's son.

The Extraverted Sensation Type

Two new guests arrive—a leading industrialist and his wife. He is an extraverted sensation type with auxiliary thinking. His wife is an introverted feeling type with intuition as an auxiliary function. This couple illustrates how individuals with opposite dominant functions often attract and complement each other.[2]

The industrialist has good common sense, a positive work ethic and a practical, enterprising nature. He knows how to handle himself in any situation. An intelligent and authoritative executive, he leads a whole army of employees and yet finds time to oversee every detail. It is rather astonishing to observe what he accomplishes professionally and socially in the course of a single day.

Nevertheless, at times he lacks a broad viewpoint. He lives so entirely in the moment that he cannot predict the results of his actions. Because his intuition remains undeveloped, he comprehends only what has already occurred and cannot foresee possible future dangers.

He is well dressed but lacks refinement, being loud and tactless. He seems warmhearted but is overwhelming as well. At dinner he is greedy.

None of their acquaintances understands what keeps him and his wife together. Nor does he; he only knows that from the moment he met her he was entranced, and that he could not live without her.

---

[2] [In this case, the dominant function of the man is in fact opposite to the woman's secondary function. See footnote above, page 77.—D.S.]

The Introverted Feeling Type

This woman, the industrialist's wife, is quiet and impenetrable. Her eyes have a mysterious depth. An inexhaustible topic of conversation for the hostess, who loves to analyze the relationships of others, is the powerful influence this young woman has over her husband.

This small and fragile woman seemingly does nothing to excite the amazing dependency of this heavy and insensitive man. Yet he follows her everywhere with his eyes and tries to catch hers. He asks her opinion constantly.

The explanation lies in the complementary nature of these opposite types. For this man, his wife is the bearer of those introverted depths which he has no access to within himself. For this reason she personifies the image he carries of the ideal feminine—his anima.

Introverted feeling types do not express their emotions often, but when they do it is with great power. These individuals accumulate an enormous amount of inner affect and this compressed intensity lends them a special aura, often perceived as an inviolate and mysterious strength.

Such types are often artistically gifted. This young woman has one real passion in her life—music. For her, music expresses the world of her feeling in a pure and uninterrupted form. Here she finds complete harmony uncontaminated by the worldly reality she finds so jarring.

Without her husband, however, she would have little contact with the outside world. He personifies her inner image of the ideal man—her animus.

The Introverted Thinking Type

In the meantime, a new visitor has come in. He is a professor of medicine, specializing in sleeping sickness. He is as well known for his boring lectures as for his new discoveries in his field. He has no contact with his students and dislikes sharing his ideas. Even his patients do not interest him, being nothing more than "cases" which he needs in order to pursue his research.

His handwriting is very small with a peculiar way of connecting the letters, readable only by himself and his assistant. It gives the impression of an impenetrable weaving. A despairing student once said, "This is not writing, this is knitting!"

One never sees the professor with his wife (who incidentally is an extraverted feeling type, his typological opposite). They never go out together and rumor has it that she is totally uneducated and was once his cleaning lady.

The Extraverted Intuitive Type

The last guest comes rushing in from the airport. He is an engineer, bubbling over with new ideas and drunk with their future possibilities. He is unlikely to put these ideas into action; more likely, he will inspire others to do so. At table, he talks enthusiastically about new travel plans, which seem over-adventurous to the host, and gobbles down his food without stopping to notice it.

The other guests are noticeably uncomfortable around this charismatic young man. He seems to be unrelated to the reality of the world they live in, but at the same time his ideas are intriguing and seductive.

The Introverted Intuitive Type

One placesetting at the table is empty—the space for the poor young poet. He neither came nor offered an explanation, he simply forgot all about it. He is a skinny young man with a fine oval face and wide, dreamy eyes.

That evening he was absorbed totally in his manuscript. Stimulated finally by hunger pangs, he went to his usual cheap restaurant. Since he has no feeling for time and space, he arrived late. (It had taken him half an hour to find his glasses before leaving.) It did not bother him that the food was mediocre. He ate his meal in an abstracted way, glancing now and then at the newspaper beside his plate.

After dinner, he went for a long walk under the starry sky, not realizing till too late that he had left his overcoat at the restaurant. Strolling along he was unaccountably inspired to create a poem—a sonnet filled with metaphysical wonders. And he was overwhelmed with joy.

All of a sudden he remembered that he had been invited to the dinner party. But it was now too late. This error, or lapse, reflected his unacknowledged feelings exactly. Though the introvert fears life's demands, there is also a touch of secret haughtiness mixed in with the shyness.

He thinks, "I shall send the lady my poem, the best I have to give." But will he really do so, or just think about it? And if he does, will the hostess understand? This poor poet, comical and grotesque in his shortsightedness and constant mishaps— this fool, who runs away from society with its joy and conflicts—may have given birth to a poem of universal meaning.

The Group

The conversation over dinner becomes quite animated. Politics, theater, sensational court cases, books and films are all discussed. The two extraverts, the lawyer and the industrialist, are involved in a heated debate.

The professor is silent. Large parties make him feel slow and awkward, and he does not enjoy these sophisticated surroundings. At the end of the meal, against his own good judgment, he suddenly breaks his silence. What does he talk about? His hobby—sleeping sickness! But since his feeling function is undeveloped and childlike, he does not realize the reactions of the other guests, nor does he sense his own inappropriateness.

The other guests respond in various ways to the professor's discourse, each for a different reason. The lawyer is always curious about noteworthy or educational ideas; the industrialist is most interested in what the professor says about the practical implementation of his work; the refined host is nauseated by the description of the illness and his digestion is upset.

But the most profound reaction is experienced by the hostess. She had tried at the beginning, unsuccessfully, to channel the professor's long monologue into a different direction. Eventually, unable to follow the conversation, she gave up. She cannot comprehend such conversation and finds it vaguely offensive. Her happy face has fallen, her eyelids are heavy and she is bored to death. Only at the end of the party, showing off her home and children to the industrialist's wife, does she regain her lively nature and happy disposition.

Index

120

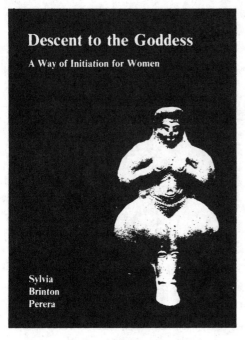

Descent to the Goddess

A Way of Initiation for Women

Sylvia
Brinton
Perera

6. Descent to the Goddess: A Way of Initiation for Women.
Sylvia Brinton Perera (New York). ISBN 0-919123-05-8. 112 pp.

A highly original and provocative book about women's freedom and the need for an inner, female authority in a masculine-oriented society.

Combining ancient texts and modern dreams, the author, a practising Jungian analyst, presents a way of feminine initiation. Inanna-Ishtar, Sumerian Goddess of Heaven and Earth, journeys into the underworld to Ereshkigal, her dark "sister," and returns. So modern women must descend from their old role-determined behavior into the depths of their instinct and image patterns, to find anew the Great Goddess and restore her values to modern culture.

Men too will be interested in this book, both for its revelations of women's essential nature and for its implications in terms of their own inner journey.

"The most significant contribution to an understanding of feminine psychology since Esther Harding's *The Way of All Women.*"—**Marion Woodman,** Jungian analyst and author of *Addiction to Perfection, The Pregnant Virgin* and *The Owl Was a Baker's Daughter.*

Addiction to Perfection
The Still Unravished Bride

A Psychological Study by
Marion Woodman

12. Addiction to Perfection: The Still Unravished Bride.
Marion Woodman (Toronto). ISBN 0-919123-11-2. 208 pp.

"This book is about taking the head off an evil witch." With these words Marion Woodman begins her spiral journey, a powerful and authoritative look at the psychology and attitudes of modern woman.

The witch is a Medusa or a Lady Macbeth, an archetypal pattern functioning autonomously in women, petrifying their spirit and inhibiting their development as free and creatively receptive individuals. Much of this, according to the author, is due to a cultural one-sidedness that favors patriarchal values—productivity, goal orientation, intellectual excellence, spiritual perfection, etc.—at the expense of more earthy, interpersonal values that have traditionally been recognized as the heart of the feminine.

Marion Woodman's first book, *The Owl Was a Baker's Daughter: Obesity, Anorexia Nervosa and the Repressed Feminine,* focused on the psychology of eating disorders and weight disturbances.

Here, with a broader perspective on the same general themes, she continues her remarkable exploration of women's mysteries through case material, dreams, literature and mythology, in food rituals, rape symbolism, Christianity, imagery in the body, sexuality, creativity and relationships.

"It is like finding the loose end in a knotted mass of thread. . . . What a relief! Somebody knows!"—**Elizabeth Strahan**, *Psychological Perspectives.*

Studies in Jungian Psychology
by Jungian Analysts

Quality Paperbacks

Prices and payment in $US (except in Canada, $Cdn)

1. The Secret Raven: Conflict and Transformation
Daryl Sharp (Toronto). ISBN 0-919123-00-7. 128 pp. $18

2. The Psychological Meaning of Redemption Motifs in Fairy Tales
Marie-Louise von Franz (Zürich). ISBN 0-919123-01-5. 128 pp. $18

3. On Divination and Synchronicity: The Psychology of Meaningful Chance
Marie-Louise von Franz (Zürich). ISBN 0-919123-02-3. 128 pp. $18

4. The Owl Was a Baker's Daughter: Obesity, Anorexia and the Repressed Feminine Marion Woodman (Toronto). ISBN 0-919123-03-1. 144 pp. $18

5. Alchemy: An Introduction to the Symbolism and the Psychology
Marie-Louise von Franz (Zürich). ISBN 0-919123-04-X. 288 pp. $25

6. Descent to the Goddess: A Way of Initiation for Women
Sylvia Brinton Perera (New York). ISBN 0-919123-05-8. 112 pp. $18

8. Border Crossings: Carlos Castaneda's Path of Knowledge
Donald Lee Williams (Boulder). ISBN 0-919123-07-4. 160 pp. $18

9. Narcissism and Character Transformation: The Psychology of Narcissistic Character Disorders
Nathan Schwartz-Salant (New York). ISBN 0-919123-08-2. 192 pp. $20

11. Alcoholism and Women: The Background and the Psychology
Jan Bauer (Montreal). ISBN 0-919123-10-4. 144 pp. $18

12. Addiction to Perfection: The Still Unravished Bride
Marion Woodman (Toronto). ISBN 0-919123-11-2. 208 pp. $20

13. Jungian Dream Interpretation: A Handbook of Theory and Practice
James A. Hall, M.D. (Dallas). ISBN 0-919123-12-0. 128 pp. $18

14. The Creation of Consciousness: Jung's Myth for Modern Man
Edward F. Edinger (Los Angeles). ISBN 0-919123-13-9. 128 pp. $18

15. The Analytic Encounter: Transference and Human Relationship
Mario Jacoby (Zürich). ISBN 0-919123-14-7. 128 pp. $18

17. The Illness That We Are: A Jungian Critique of Christianity
John P. Dourley (Ottawa). ISBN 0-919123-16-3. 128 pp. $18

19. Cultural Attitudes in Psychological Perspective
Joseph L. Henderson, M.D. (San Francisco). ISBN 0-919123-18-X. 128 pp. $18

21. The Pregnant Virgin: A Process of Psychological Transformation
Marion Woodman (Toronto). ISBN 0-919123-20-1. 208 pp. $20

22. Encounter with the Self: A Jungian Commentary on William Blake's *Illustrations of the Book of Job*
Edward F. Edinger (Los Angeles). ISBN 0-919123-21-X. 80 pp. $18

23. The Scapegoat Complex: Toward a Mythology of Shadow and Guilt
Sylvia Brinton Perera (New York). ISBN 0-919123-22-8. 128 pp. $18

24. The Bible and the Psyche: Individuation Symbolism in the Old Testament
Edward F. Edinger (Los Angeles). ISBN 0-919123-23-6. 176 pp. $20

26. The Jungian Experience: Analysis and Individuation
James A. Hall, M.D. (Dallas). ISBN 0-919123-25-2. 176 pp. $20

27. Phallos: Sacred Image of the Masculine
Eugene Monick (Scranton, PA). ISBN 0-919123-26-0. 144 pp. $18

28. The Christian Archetype: A Jungian Commentary on the Life of Christ
Edward F. Edinger (Los Angeles). ISBN 0-919123-27-9. 144 pp. $18

30. Touching: Body Therapy and Depth Psychology
Deldon Anne McNeely (Lynchburg, VA). ISBN 0-919123-29-5. 128 pp. $18

31. Personality Types: Jung's Model of Typology
Daryl Sharp (Toronto). ISBN 0-919123-30-9. 128 pp. $18

32. The Sacred Prostitute: Eternal Aspect of the Feminine
Nancy Qualls-Corbett (Birmingham). ISBN 0-919123-31-7. 176 pp. $20

33. When the Spirits Come Back
Janet O. Dallett (Seal Harbor, WA). ISBN 0-919123-32-5. 160 pp. $18

34. The Mother: Archetypal Image in Fairy Tales
Sibylle Birkhäuser-Oeri (Zürich). ISBN 0-919123-33-3. 176 pp. $20

35. The Survival Papers: Anatomy of a Midlife Crisis
Daryl Sharp (Toronto). ISBN 0-919123-34-1. 160 pp. $18

37. Dear Gladys: The Survival Papers, Book 2
Daryl Sharp (Toronto). ISBN 0-919123-36-8. 144 pp. $18

39. Acrobats of the Gods: Dance and Transformation
Joan Dexter Blackmer (Wilmot Flat, NH). ISBN 0-919123-38-4. 128 pp. $18

40. Eros and Pathos: Shades of Love and Suffering
Aldo Carotenuto (Rome). ISBN 0-919123-39-2. 160 pp. $18

41. The Ravaged Bridegroom: Masculinity in Women
Marion Woodman (Toronto). ISBN 0-919123-42-2. 224 pp. $22

43. Goethe's *Faust:* Notes for a Jungian Commentary
Edward F. Edinger (Los Angeles). ISBN 0-919123-44-9. 112 pp. $18

44. The Dream Story
Donald Broadribb (Baker's Hill, Australia). ISBN 0-919123-45-7. 256 pp. $24

45. The Rainbow Serpent: Bridge to Consciousness
Robert L. Gardner (Toronto). ISBN 0-919123-46-5. 128 pp. $18

46. Circle of Care: Clinical Issues in Jungian Therapy
Warren Steinberg (New York). ISBN 0-919123-47-3. 160 pp. $18

47. Jung Lexicon: A Primer of Terms & Concepts
Daryl Sharp (Toronto). ISBN 0-919123-48-1. 160 pp. $18

48. Body and Soul: The Other Side of Illness
Albert Kreinheder (Los Angeles). ISBN 0-919123-49-X. 112 pp. $18

49. Animus Aeternus: Exploring the Inner Masculine
Deldon Anne McNeely (Lynchburg, VA). ISBN 0-919123-50-3. 192 pp. $20

50. Castration and Male Rage: The Phallic Wound
Eugene Monick (Scranton, PA). ISBN 0-919123-51-1. 144 pp. $18

51. Saturday's Child: Encounters with the Dark Gods
Janet O. Dallett (Seal Harbor, WA). ISBN 0-919123-52-X. 128 pp. $16

52. The Secret Lore of Gardening: Patterns of Male Intimacy
Graham Jackson (Toronto). ISBN 0-919123-53-8. 160 pp. $16

53. The Refiner's Fire: Memoirs of a German Girlhood
Sigrid R. McPherson (Los Angeles). ISBN 0-919123-54-6. 208 pp. $18

54. Transformation of the God-Image: Jung's *Answer to Job*
Edward F. Edinger (Los Angeles). ISBN 0-919123-55-4. 144 pp. $18

55. Getting to Know You: The Inside Out of Relationship
Daryl Sharp (Toronto). ISBN 0-919123-56-2. 128 pp. $18

56. A Strategy for a Loss of Faith: Jung's Proposal
John P. Dourley (Ottawa). ISBN 0-919123-57-0. 144 pp. $18

58. Conscious Femininity: Interviews with Marion Woodman
Introduction by Marion Woodman (Toronto). ISBN 0-919123-59-7. 160 pp. $18

59. The Middle Passage: From Misery to Meaning in Midlife
James Hollis (Houston). ISBN 0-919123-60-0. 128 pp. $18

60. The Living Room Mysteries: Patterns of Male Intimacy, Book 2
Graham Jackson (Toronto). ISBN 0-919123-61-9. 144 pp. $18

61. Chicken Little: The Inside Story *(A Jungian Romance)*
Daryl Sharp (Toronto). ISBN 0-919123-62-7. 128 pp. $18

62. Coming To Age: The Croning Years and Late-Life Transformation
Jane R. Prétat (Providence, RI). ISBN 0-919123-63-5. 144 pp. $18

63. Under Saturn's Shadow: The Wounding and Healing of Men
James Hollis (Houston). ISBN 0-919123-64-3. 144 pp. $18

65. The Mystery of the Coniunctio: Alchemical Image of Individuation
Edward F. Edinger (Los Angeles). ISBN 0-919123-67-8. 112 pp. $18

66. The Mysterium Lectures: Journey through Jung's *Mysterium Coniunctionis*
Edward F. Edinger (Los Angeles). ISBN 0-919123-66-X. 352 pp. $30

83. The Cat: A Tale of Feminine Redemption
Marie-Louise von Franz (Zurich). ISBN 0-919123-84-8. 128 pp. $18

87. The Problem of the Puer Aeternus
Marie-Louise von Franz (Zurich). ISBN 0-919123-88-0. 288 pp. $25

95. Digesting Jung: Food for the Journey
Daryl Sharp (Toronto). ISBN 0-919123-96-1. 128 pp. $18

99. The Secret World of Drawings: Healing through Art
Gregg M. Furth (New York). ISBN 1-894574-00-1. 100 illustrations. 176 pp. $25

100. Animus and Anima in Fairy Tales
Marie-Louise von Franz (Zurich). ISBN 1-894574-01-X. 128 pp. $18

108. The Sacred Psyche: A Psychological Approach to the Psalms
Edward F. Edinger (Los Angeles). ISBN 1-894574-09-5. 160 pp. $18

111. The Secret Garden: Temenos for Individuation
Margaret Eileen Meredith (Toronto). ISBN 1-894574-12-5. 160 pp. $18

112. Not the Big Sleep: on having fun, seriously *(A Jungian Romance)*
Daryl Sharp (Toronto). ISBN 1-894574-13-3. 128 pp. $18

113. The Use of Dreams in Couple Counseling
Renée Nell (Litchfield, CT). ISBN 1-894574-14-1. 160 pp. $18

Discounts: *any 3-5 books, 10%; 6-9 books, 20%; 10 or more, 25%*

Add Postage/Handling: 1-2 books, $6 surface ($10 air); 3-4 books, $8 surface ($12 air); 5-9 books, $15 surface ($20 air); 10 or more, $10 surface ($25 air)

Free Catalogue of **over 100 titles** and **Jung at Heart** newsletter

INNER CITY BOOKS, Box 1271, Station Q, Toronto, ON M4T 2P4, Canada
Tel. 416- 927-0355 / Fax 416-924-1814 / E-mail: sales@innercitybooks.net